Crocheted Beanies & Slouchy Hats

31 Patterns for Fun Colorful Hats

JULIE KING

STACKPOLE BOOKS

Guilford, Connecticut

Published by Stackpole Books
An imprint of The Rowman & Littlefield Publishing Group, Inc.
4501 Forbes Blvd., Ste. 200
Lanham, MD 20706
www.stackpolebooks.com

Distributed by NATIONAL BOOK NETWORK
800-462-6420

British Library Cataloguing in Publication Information available

Library of Congress Cataloging-in-Publication Data

Names: King, Julie (Crochet designer), author.
Title: Crocheted beanies and slouchy hats : 31 patterns for fun colorful hats / Julie King.
Description: First edition. | Guilford, Connecticut : Stackpole Books, 2019.
   | Includes index.
Identifiers: LCCN 2018025573 (print) | LCCN 2018026522 (ebook) | ISBN 9780811767583
   (ebook) | ISBN 9780811717960 (pbk. : alk. paper)
Subjects: LCSH: Crocheting—Patterns. | Hats.
Classification: LCC TT825 (ebook) | LCC TT825 .K57 2019 (print) | DDC 746.43/4—dc23
LC record available at https://lccn.loc.gov/2018025573

♾™ The paper used in this publication meets the minimum requirements of American National Standard for Information Sciences—Permanence of Paper for Printed Library Materials, ANSI/NISO Z39.48-1992.

First Edition

Printed in the United States of America

Contents

Introduction

Some of my favorite crochet projects are the ones that are quick to make, not too difficult, and fun to wear. My goal was to create a collection of patterns that would embody all of those attributes.

Within these pages, you'll find three types of hats in a variety of yarn weights, ranging from #4 medium worsted weight to #6 super bulky weight. First, we have beanies, which are classic but anything but basic! Next, there are the always popular slouchy hats, which start out as a large circle that eventually decreases in size to fit around your head. And finally, there is my personal favorite: slouchy beanies, which are very similar to a normal beanie but are slouchy due to being extra long. Whichever style is your favorite, I've included a number of each for you to choose from.

The patterns are ranked from beginner to easy to intermediate. If you find instructions you're unfamiliar with, see the "Stitches and Techniques" section at the end of this book; it features photo tutorials to help you out. Because I wanted to ensure that all of these hats were fairly beginner-friendly, I thought back to when I was a beginner and tried to recall my favorite stitches, techniques, and yarns.

When I first learned to crochet, I was fresh out of college and, needless to say, on a tight budget. One of the things that appealed to me about crochet was how affordable a hobby it could be. I quickly came to appreciate yarns that I could get at my local craft stores as well as projects that could be completed with a single skein. I kept those aspects in mind while creating this collection of patterns, and I focused on using yarns that are easily obtainable locally or online. I even included several one-skein hats!

That said, another thing that is great about crochet is that you can take a simple project like a hat and make it feel more extravagant by using a fancy yarn or adding embellishments. I encourage you to experiment with yarns you may not have tried yet and to give your hats a little something extra by adding buttons, pom-poms, or ribbon. It's your yarn choices and those little finishing touches that make your projects unique!

I hope you have lots of fun working with these patterns and find your new favorite hat within these pages. Happy crocheting!

Patterns

Seashell Slouchy Hat

Seashell Slouchy Hat

A classy, slouchy hat that looks great with a casual outfit or slightly dressed up! Use one or two colors to stitch one up to suit your style.

YARN

Bernat Satin, #4 medium worsted weight yarn, acrylic, 3.5 oz (100 g) per skein: 190 yd (174 m) of #04021 Linen (**A**) and 20 yd (18 m) of #04013 Mocha (**B**)

MATERIALS

» US Size I/9 (5.5 mm) crochet hook or size needed to obtain gauge
» Yarn needle
» Scissors

DIFFICULTY

Easy

SIZES

One size

FINISHED MEASUREMENTS

Length: 10 in (25 cm)
Circumference: 20 in (51 cm)

GAUGE

[1 FPdc in next st, 3 dc in next ch space, ch 1, 3 dc in same ch space] 2 times and 6 rows = 4 in (10 cm)

NOTES

» Pattern is worked in joined rounds.
» With the exception of round 1, chs at the beginning of rounds do not count as a stitch. When joining at the end of the round, skip the ch and join to the first st.

INSTRUCTIONS

With A, make a magic ring.

Round 1: Ch 3 (counts as 1 dc), 11 dc in ring, sl st to top of ch 3 to join—12 dc.

Round 2: Ch 2 (does not count as a st now and throughout), 1 FPdc, 1 dc in same st, *1 FPdc in next st, 1 dc in same st; repeat from * around, sl st to 1st FPdc to join—12 FPdc + 12 dc.

Round 3: Ch 2, 1 FPdc, ch1, 1 dc in next st, *1 FPdc in next st, ch 1, 1 dc in next st; repeat from * around, sl st to 1st FPdc to join—12 FPdc + 12 ch-1 spaces + 12 dc.

Round 4: Ch 2, 1 FPdc, 1 dc in next ch space, ch 1, 1 dc in same ch space, *1 FPdc in next st, 1 dc in next ch space, ch 1, 1 dc in same ch space; repeat from * around, sl st to 1st FPdc to join—12 FPdc + 12 ch-1 spaces + 24 dc.

Round 5: Ch 2, 1 FPdc, 1 dc in next ch space, ch 1, 2 dc in same ch space, *1 FPdc in next st, 1 dc in next ch space, ch 1, 2 dc in same ch space; repeat from * around, sl st to 1st FPdc to join—12 FPdc + 12 ch-1 spaces + 36 dc.

Round 6: Ch 2, 1 FPdc, 2 dc in next ch space, ch 1, 2 dc in same ch space, *1 FPdc in next st, 2 dc in next ch space, ch 1, 2 dc in same ch space; repeat from * around, sl st to 1st FPdc to join—12 FPdc + 12 ch-1 spaces + 48 dc.

Round 7: Ch 2, 1 FPdc, 2 dc in next ch space, ch 1, 3 dc in same ch space, *1 FPdc in next st, 2 dc in next ch space, ch 1, 3 dc in same ch space; repeat from * around, sl st to 1st FPdc to join—12 FPdc + 12 ch-1 spaces + 60 dc.

Rounds 8–15: Ch 2, 1 FPdc, 3 dc in next ch space, ch 1, 3 dc in same ch space, *1 FPdc in next st, 3 dc in next ch space, ch 1, 3 dc in same ch space; repeat from * around, sl st to 1st FPdc to join—12 FPdc + 12 ch-1 spaces + 72 dc.

Round 16: Ch 2, 1 FPdc, 2 dc in next ch space, ch 1, 2 dc in same ch space, *1 FPdc in next st, 2 dc in next ch space, ch 1, 2 dc in same ch space; repeat from * around, sl st to 1st FPdc to join, and fasten off **A**—12 FPdc + 12 ch-1 spaces + 48 dc.

Round 17: With **B**, ch 2, 1 FPdc, 2 dc in next ch space, ch 1, 2 dc in same ch space, *1 FPdc in next st, 2 dc in next ch space, ch 1, 2 dc in same ch space; repeat from * around, sl st to 1st FPdc to join—12 FPdc + 12 ch-1 spaces + 48 dc.

Round 18: Ch 2, 1 FPdc, 2 dc in next ch space, ch 1, 2 dc in same ch space, *1 FPdc in next st, 2 dc in next ch space, ch 1, 2 dc in same ch space; repeat from * around, invisible join to 1st FPdc, and fasten off **B**—12 FPdc + 12 ch-1 spaces + 48 dc.

Lakeshore Beanie

This cozy beanie uses the linen stitch, which looks great with an ombre yarn! A large faux flap and two big buttons on the side complete this casual look.

YARN
Lion Brand Yarns Scarfie, #5 bulky weight yarn, acrylic/wool, 5.3 oz (150 g) per skein: 120 yd (110 m) of #215 Cream/Teal

MATERIALS
» US Size K/10.5 (6.5 mm) crochet hook or size needed to obtain gauge
» Yarn needle
» Scissors
» Stitch marker
» Two 1½ in (4 cm) buttons

DIFFICULTY
Beginner

SIZES
One size

FINISHED MEASUREMENTS
Length: 7½ in (19 cm)
Circumference: 20 in (51 cm)

GAUGE
[Sc, ch 1] 7 times and 14 rows = 4 in (10 cm)

NOTES
» Top portion of hat is worked in continuous rounds without joining. Use a stitch marker to mark the first stitch of each round.
» Flap portion of hat is worked in rows, turning at each end.
» Ch 2 at beginning of rows will always count as 1 sc + 1 ch space.

INSTRUCTIONS

Make a magic ring.

Round 1: Ch 1 (does not count as a st), [1 sc in ring, ch 1] 5 times—5 sc + 5 ch-1 spaces.

Round 2: *1 sc in next ch space, ch 1, 1 sc in same ch space, ch 1; repeat from * around—10 sc + 10 ch-1 spaces.

Round 3: *[1 sc in next ch space, ch 1] 2 times, 1 sc in same ch space, ch 1; repeat from * around—15 sc + 15 ch-1 spaces.

Round 4: *[1 sc in next ch space, ch 1] 3 times, 1 sc in same ch space, ch 1; repeat from * around—20 sc + 20 ch-1 spaces.

Round 5: *[1 sc in next ch space, ch 1] 4 times, 1 sc in same ch space, ch 1; repeat from * around—25 sc + 25 ch-1 spaces.

Round 6: *[1 sc in next ch space, ch 1] 5 times, 1 sc in same ch space, ch 1; repeat from * around—30 sc + 30 ch-1 spaces.

Round 7: *[1 sc in next ch space, ch 1] 6 times, 1 sc in same ch space, ch 1; repeat from * around—35 sc + 35 ch-1 spaces.

Rounds 8–11: *1 sc in next ch space, ch 1; repeat from * around—35 sc + 35 ch-1 spaces.

Leave st marker in place after round 11. Begin working in rows, turning.

Round 12: Ch 9 (final 2 count as 1 sc + 1 ch space) and turn, 1 sc in 3rd ch from hook, ch 1, [skip 1 ch, 1 sc in next ch, ch 1] 3 times, 1 sc in next ch space, *ch 1, 1 sc in next ch space; repeat from * around until st marker—39 sc + 38 ch-1 spaces.

Rounds 13–25: Ch 2 (will count as 1 sc + 1 ch space now and throughout) and turn, 1 sc in next ch space, *ch 1, sc in next ch space; repeat from * across—39 sc + 38 ch-1 spaces.

EDGING

Ch 1, 1 sc in same ch space as last sc, ch 1 *skip 1 row, 1 sc in end of next row, ch 1; repeat from * until next corner, 1 sc in same ch space as last sc, ch 1; **skip next st, 1 sc in next ch space; repeat from ** until st marker, fasten off, leaving a long tail for finishing.

FINISHING

Use long tail and yarn needle to stitch flap down. Attach buttons to flap.

Diamonds Slouchy Hat

A unique slouchy hat that is light and airy, making it a perfect accessory for less chilly days. As you crochet, you'll see a diamond pattern form in the openings!

YARN
Caron Simply Soft, #4 medium worsted weight yarn, acrylic, 6 oz (170 g) per skein: 200 yd (182 m) of #9722 Plum Wine

MATERIALS
» US Size J/10 (6 mm) crochet hook or size needed to obtain gauge
» Yarn needle
» Scissors

DIFFICULTY
Easy

SIZES
One size

FINISHED MEASUREMENTS
Length: 12 in (30 cm)
Circumference: 19 in (48 cm)

GAUGE
12 dc and 6 rows = 4 in (10 cm)

NOTES
» Ch 4 at beginning of rounds will always count as 1 dc + 1 ch.
» Pattern is worked in joined rounds with the exception of rounds 19 and 21, where joining is not necessary.
» Rounds 20 and 22 will be worked into the round before the previous, in the same sts where the sl sts are worked.
» When instructed to "sc in ch space 2 rounds below," you will make your sc around the ch space in the previous round as well as into the ch space 2 rounds below.

INSTRUCTIONS

Make a magic ring.

Round 1: Ch 5 (counts as 1 tr + 1 ch), [1 tr in ring, ch 1] 11 times, sl st to 4th ch to join—12 tr + 12 ch-1 spaces.

Round 2: Sl st into next ch space, ch 4 (counts as 1 dc + 1 ch now and throughout), 1 dc in same ch space, ch 1, *[1 dc, ch 1, 1 dc] in next ch space, ch 1; repeat from * around, sl st to 3rd ch to join—24 dc + 24 ch-1 spaces.

Round 3: Sl st into next ch space, ch 4, 2 dc in same ch space, ch 1, skip 1 ch space, *[2 dc, ch 1, 2 dc] in next ch space, ch 1, skip 1 ch space; repeat from * around, 1 dc in same ch space as beginning ch 4, sl st to 3rd ch to join—48 dc + 24 ch-1 spaces.

Round 4: Sl st into next ch space, ch 4, 2 dc in same ch space, ch 1, 1 sc in ch space 2 rounds below, ch 1, *[2 dc, ch 1, 2 dc] in next ch space, ch 1, 1 sc in ch space 2 rounds below, ch 1; repeat from * around, 1 dc in same ch space as beginning ch 4, sl st to 3rd ch to join—48 dc + 36 ch-1 spaces + 12 sc.

Round 5: Sl st into next ch space, ch 4, 3 dc in same ch space, ch 2, skip 2 ch-1 spaces, *[3 dc, ch 1, 3 dc] in next ch-1 space, ch 2, skip 2 ch-1 spaces; repeat from * around, 2 dc in same ch space as beginning ch 4, sl st to 3rd ch to join—72 dc + 12 ch-1 spaces + 12 ch-2 spaces.

Round 6: Sl st into next ch space, ch 4, 3 dc in same ch space, ch 2, skip 2 ch spaces, *[3 dc, ch 1, 3 dc] in next ch-1 space, ch 2, skip 2 ch spaces; repeat from * around, 2 dc in same ch space as beginning ch 4, sl st to 3rd ch to join—72 dc +12 ch-1 spaces + 12 ch-2 spaces.

Round 7: Sl st into next ch space, ch 4, 3 dc in same ch space, ch 1, 1 sc in ch-2 space 2 rounds below, ch 1, *[3 dc, ch 1, 3 dc] in next ch space, ch 1, 1 sc in ch space 2 rounds below, ch 1; repeat from * around, 2 dc in same ch space as beginning ch 4, sl st to 3rd ch to join—72 dc + 36 ch-1 spaces + 12 sc.

Rounds 8–16: Repeat rounds 5–7.

Round 17: Sl st into next ch space, ch 1 (does not count as a st), 4 sc in same ch space, ch 2, skip 2 ch-1 spaces, *4 sc in next ch space, ch 2, skip 2 ch-1 spaces; repeat from * around, sl st to 1st sc to join—48 sc + 12 ch-2 spaces.

Round 18: Ch 1 (does not count as a st), *1 sc in each of the next 4 sc, 2 sc in next ch-2 space; repeat from * around, sl st to 1st sc to join—72 sc.

Round 19: 1 sl st in each st around; do not join—72 sl st.

Round 20: Sl st into 1st st of round 18, ch 1 (does not count as a st), 1 sc in each st around, working into round 18, sl st to join to 1st sc—72 sc.

Round 21: Repeat round 19.

Round 22: Sl st into 1st st of round 20, ch 1 (does not count as a st), 1 sc in each st around, working into round 20, invisible join to 1st sc, and fasten off—72 sc.

Pumpkin Pie Slouchy Beanie

Pumpkin Pie Slouchy Beanie

This one-skein slouchy beanie features an easy cable around the edge and a fun pom-pom on top. If you've never tried crochet cables, this is the perfect first project!

YARN
Patons Alpaca Blend, #5 bulky weight yarn, acrylic/wool/nylon/alpaca, 3.5 oz (100 g) per skein: 155 yd (142 m) of #01023 Butternut

MATERIALS
» US Size J/10 (6 mm) crochet hook or size needed to obtain gauge
» Yarn needle
» Scissors
» Faux fur pom-pom

DIFFICULTY
Intermediate

SIZES
One size

FINISHED MEASUREMENTS
Length: 10 in (25 cm)
Circumference: 20 in (51 cm)

GAUGE
[2 hdc, ch 1] 4 times and 8 rows = 4 in (10 cm)

NOTES
» Edging of hat is worked flat in rows and then stitched together to form a band. Body of hat is then worked in joined rounds into the side of the edging.
» Ch 1 in beginning of rows/rounds always counts as 1 hdc.

INSTRUCTIONS

EDGING

Row 1 (RS): Ch 11 (2 count as 1 hdc), 1 hdc in 3rd ch from hook and in each ch across—10 hdc.

Row 2: Ch 1 (counts as 1 hdc now and throughout) and turn, 1 hdc in each st across—10 hdc.

Row 3: Ch 1 and turn, 1 hdc in each of the next 2 sts, 1 FPtr in each of the next 4 sts 2 rows below, 1 hdc in each of the next 3 sts—6 hdc + 4 FPtr.

Row 4: Ch 1 and turn, 1 hdc in each st across— 10 hdc.

Row 5: Ch 1 and turn, 1 hdc in each of the next 2 sts, skip 2 sts, 1 FPtr in each of the next 2 sts 2 rows below, 1 FPtr in each of the 2 skipped sts 2 rows below, 1 hdc in each of the next 3 sts—6 hdc + 4 FPtr.

Row 6: Ch 1 and turn, 1 hdc in each st across— 10 hdc.

Rows 7–46: Repeat rows 3–6.

Rows 47–49: Repeat rows 3–5.

Cut yarn, leaving a long tail. Using your yarn needle and the tail, stitch final row to beginning chain to form a band, and fasten off.

BODY OF HAT

Begin in last st of row 49, working in edge of band with RS facing you.

Round 1: Ch 1 (counts as 1 hdc now and through-out), 1 hdc in same st, ch 1, *skip 1 row, 2 hdc in next row, ch 1; repeat from * around, sl st to 1st hdc to join—50 hdc + 25 ch-1 spaces.

Round 2: Sl st into next ch space, ch 1, 1 hdc in same ch space, ch 1, *2 hdc in next ch space, ch 1; repeat from * around, sl st to 1st hdc to join—50 hdc + 25 ch-1 spaces.

Rounds 3–8: Repeat round 2.

Round 9: Sl st into next ch space, ch 1, 1 hdc in same ch space, 2 hdc in each ch space around, sl st to 1st hdc to join—50 hdc.

Rounds 10–11: Sl st into next space after 1st 2 hdc of previous round, ch 1, 1 hdc in same space, *2 hdc in space after next 2 sts; repeat from * around, sl st to 1st hdc to join—50 hdc.

Round 12: Sl st into next space after 1st 2 hdc of previous round, ch 1, *1 hdc in space after next 2 sts; repeat from * around, sl st to ch 1 to join—25 hdc.

Round 13: Sl st into next space after ch 1 of previous round, ch 1, *1 hdc in space after next st; repeat from * around, sl st to ch 1 to join—25 hdc.

Cut yarn, leaving a long tail. Using your yarn needle and the tail, stitch around round 13. Pull tight to cinch shut, and fasten off.

Attach a faux fur pom-pom if desired.

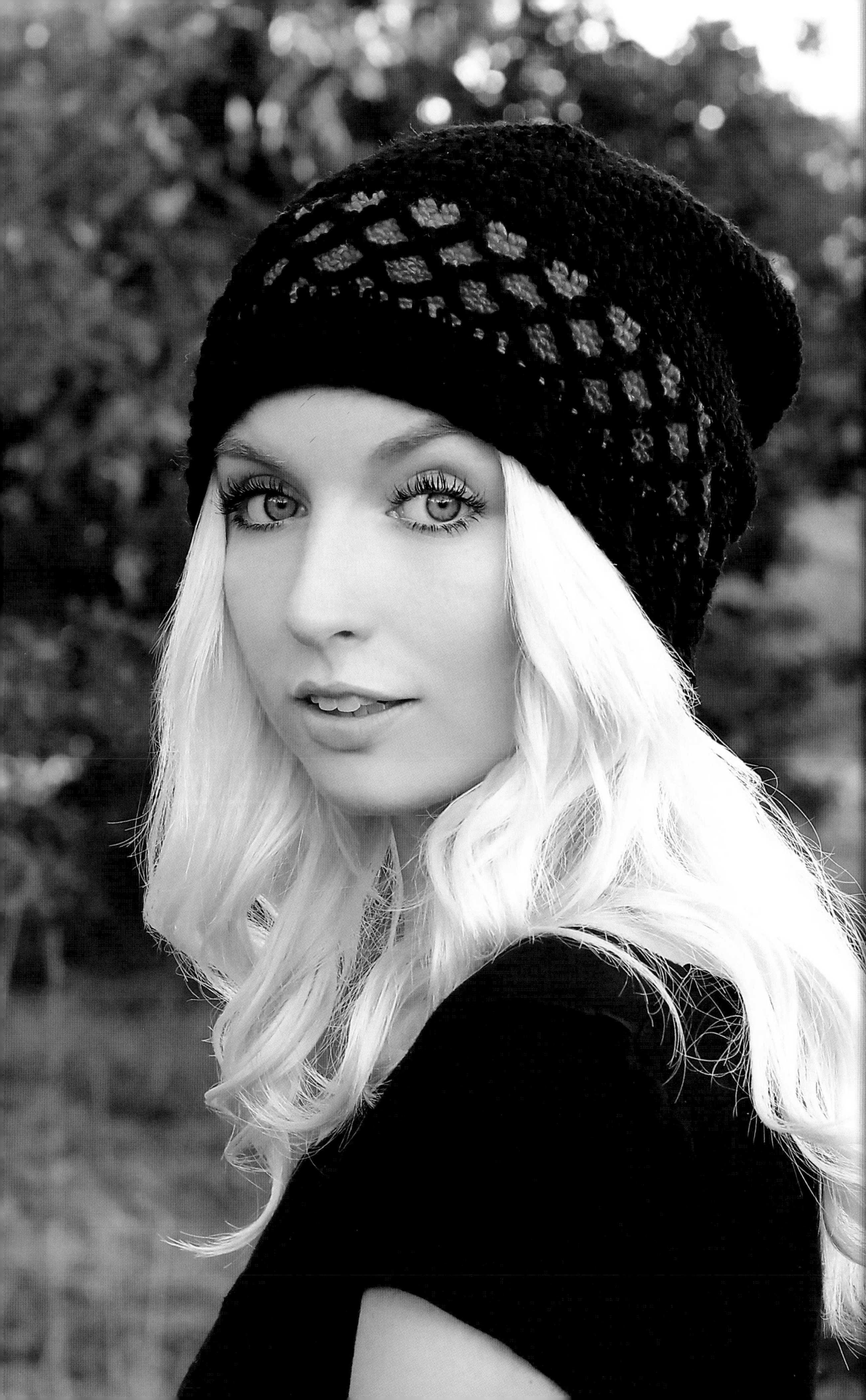

Stained Glass Slouchy Beanie

Stained Glass Slouchy Beanie

This slouchy beanie uses two layers of stitches to create a look similar to stained glass. Use your favorite ombre yarn along with a solid color to craft your own unique look!

YARN
Knit Picks Chroma, #4 medium worsted weight yarn, wool/nylon, 3.5 oz (100 g) per skein: 140 yd (128 m) of #25885 Black (**A**) and 50 yd (46 m) of #26471 Lupine (**B**)

MATERIALS
» US Size H/8 (5 mm) crochet hook or size needed to obtain gauge
» Yarn needle
» Scissors

DIFFICULTY
Easy

SIZES
One size

FINISHED MEASUREMENTS
Length: 10 in (25 cm)
Circumference: 20 in (51 cm)

GAUGE
14 dc and 7 rows = 4 in (10 cm)

NOTES
» Ch 1 at beginning of rounds never counts as a st.
» Ch 3 at beginning of rounds always counts as 1 dc.
» In round 16, you will be working into round 12. Rounds 16–26 will be behind rounds 13–15. In round 27, you will be instructed to make some sts going through both a ch-5 space from round 15 and a sc in round 26.

With **A**, make a magic ring.

Round 1: Ch 3 (counts as 1 dc now and throughout), 11 dc in ring, sl st to join to 1st dc—12 dc.

Round 2: Ch 3, 1 dc in same st, 2 dc in each st around, sl st to join to 1st dc—24 dc.

Round 3: Ch 3, 2 dc in next st, *1 dc in next st, 2 dc in next st; repeat from * around, sl st to join to 1st dc—36 dc.

Round 4: Ch 3, 1 dc in next st, 2 dc in next st, *1 dc in each of the next 2 sts, 2 dc in next st; repeat from * around, sl st to join to 1st dc—48 dc.

Round 5: Ch 3, 1 dc in each of the next 2 sts, 2 dc in next st, *1 dc in each of the next 3 sts, 2 dc in next st; repeat from * around, sl st to join to 1st dc—60 dc.

Round 6: Ch 3, 1 dc in each of the next 3 sts, 2 dc in next st, *1 dc in each of the next 4 sts, 2 dc in next st; repeat from * around, sl st to join to 1st dc—72 dc.

Rounds 7–12: Ch 3, 1 dc in each st around, sl st to join to 1st dc—72 dc.

Round 13: Ch 1 (does not count as a st now and throughout), 1 FLO sc in same st, ch 5, skip 2 sts, *1 FLO sc in next st, ch 5, skip 2 sts; repeat from * around, sl st to join to 1st sc—24 sc + 24 ch-5 spaces.

Round 14: Sl st into next ch space, ch 1, 1 sc in same ch space, ch 5, *1 sc in next ch space, ch 5; repeat from * around, sl st to join to 1st sc—24 sc + 24 ch-5 spaces.

Round 15: Sl st into next ch space, ch 1, 1 sc in same ch space, ch 5, *1 sc in next ch space, ch 5; repeat from * around, invisible join to 1st sc, and fasten off **A**—24 sc + 24 ch-5 spaces.

Round 16: With **B**, ch 1 in BLO in 1st st of round 12, 1 BLO sc in same st, 1 sc in each of the next 2 sts, *1 BLO sc in next st, 1 sc in each of the next 2 sts; repeat from * around, sl st to join to 1st sc—72 sc.

Rounds 17–26: Ch 1, 1 sc in each st around, sl st to join to 1st sc—72 sc.

Round 27: With **A**, ch 3 and fasten off **B**, 1 dc going through next ch-5 space from round 15 and next sc from round 26, *1 dc in each of the next 2 sc, 1 dc going through next ch-5 space and next sc; repeat from * around, 1 dc in next sc, sl st to join to 1st dc—72 dc.

Round 28: Ch 3, 1 FPdc in next st, *1 dc in next st, 1 FPdc in next st; repeat from * around, sl st to join to 1st dc—36 dc + 36 FPdc.

Round 29: Ch 3, 1 FPdc in next st, *1 dc in next st, 1 FPdc in next st; repeat from * around, invisible join 1st dc, and fasten off **A**—36 dc + 36 FPdc.

Ferris Wheel Slouchy Hat

Ferris Wheel Slouchy Hat

A simple, ribbed slouchy hat is sure to become a staple in your wardrobe. It looks great in solid or multitonal colors and can be made with just one skein!

YARN
Knit Picks Preciosa Tonal, #4 medium worsted weight yarn, merino wool, 3.5 oz (100 g) per skein: 220 yd (201 m) of #26728 Boysenberry

MATERIALS
» US Size H/8 (5 mm) crochet hook or size needed to obtain gauge
» Yarn needle
» Scissors

DIFFICULTY
Intermediate

SIZES
One size

FINISHED MEASUREMENTS
Length: 9 in (23 cm)
Circumference: 20 in (51 cm)

GAUGE
12 dc and 8 rows = 4 in (10 cm)

NOTES
» Pattern is worked in joined rounds.
» With the exception of round 1, chs at the beginning of rounds do not count as a stitch. When joining at the end of the round, skip the ch and join to the first st.

INSTRUCTIONS

Make a magic ring.

Round 1: Ch 3 (counts as 1 dc), 13 dc in ring, sl st to top of 3rd ch to join—14 dc.

Round 2: Ch 2 (does not count as a st now and throughout), 2 FPdc in each st around, sl st to 1st FPdc to join—28 FPdc.

Round 3: Ch 2, *1 FPdc in each of the next 2 sts, 1 dc in same st; repeat from * around, sl st to 1st FPdc to join—28 FPdc + 14 dc.

Round 4: Ch 2, *1 FPdc in each of the next 2 sts, 1 dc in next st; repeat from * around, sl st to 1st FPdc to join—28 FPdc + 14 dc.

Round 5: Ch 2, *1 FPdc in each of the next 2 sts, 2 dc in next st; repeat from * around, sl st to 1st FPdc to join—28 FPdc + 28 dc.

Round 6: Ch 2, *1 FPdc in each of the next 2 sts, 1 dc in each of the next 2 sts; repeat from * around, sl st to 1st FPdc to join—28 FPdc + 28 dc.

Round 7: Ch 2, *1 FPdc in each of the next 2 sts, 1 dc in next st, 2 dc in next st; repeat from * around, sl st to 1st FPdc to join—28 FPdc + 42 dc.

Round 8: Ch 2, *1 FPdc in each of the next 2 sts, 1 dc in each of the next 3 sts; repeat from * around, sl st to 1st FPdc to join—28 FPdc + 42 dc.

Round 9: Ch 2, *1 FPdc in each of the next 2 sts, 1 dc in each of the next 2 sts, 2 dc in next st; repeat from * around, sl st to 1st FPdc to join—28 FPdc + 56 dc.

Round 10: Ch 2, *1 FPdc in each of the next 2 sts, 1 dc in each of the next 4 sts; repeat from * around, sl st to 1st FPdc to join—28 FPdc + 56 dc.

Round 11: Ch 2, *1 FPdc in each of the next 2 sts, 1 dc in each of the next 3 sts, 2 dc in next st; repeat from * around, sl st to 1st FPdc to join—28 FPdc + 70 dc.

Rounds 12–16: Ch 2, *1 FPdc in each of the next 2 sts, 1 dc in each of the next 5 sts; repeat from * around, sl st to 1st FPdc to join—28 FPdc + 70 dc.

Round 17: Ch 2, *1 FPdc in each of the next 2 sts, 1 dc in each of the next 3 sts, dc2tog; repeat from * around, sl st to 1st FPdc to join—28 FPdc + 42 dc + 14 dc2tog.

Rounds 18–19: Ch 2, *1 FPdc in each of the next 2 sts, 1 dc in each of the next 4 sts; repeat from * around, sl st to 1st FPdc to join—28 FPdc + 56 dc.

Round 20: Ch 2, *1 FPdc in each of the next 2 sts, 1 dc in each of the next 2 sts, dc2tog; repeat from * around, sl st to 1st FPdc to join—28 FPdc + 28 dc + 14 dc2tog.

Rounds 21–23: Ch 1 (does not count as a st), 1 sc in each st around, sl st to 1st sc to join—70 sc.

Round 24: Ch 1 (does not count as a st), 1 sc in each st around, invisible join to 1st sc, and fasten off—70 sc.

Swell Slouchy Beanie

Swell Slouchy Beanie

This slouchy beanie uses double crochets to create an easy wave pattern. Choosing a multicolored yarn is a fun way to make sure the waves really stand out!

YARN
Yarn Bee Aspyn, #5 bulky weight yarn, acrylic/alpaca, 3.5 oz (100 g) per skein: 130 yd (119 m) of #29 Mountain Bluebird

MATERIALS
» US Size K/10.5 (6.5 mm) crochet hook or size needed to obtain gauge
» Yarn needle
» Scissors

DIFFICULTY
Beginner

SIZES
One size

FINISHED MEASUREMENTS
Length: 11 in (28 cm)
Circumference: 20 in (51 cm)

GAUGE
12 dc and 5 rows = 4 in (10 cm)

NOTES
» The ch 1 at beginning of rounds never counts as a st.
» The ch 3 at beginning of rounds will always count as 1 dc.

INSTRUCTIONS

Make a magic ring.

Round 1: Ch 3 (counts as 1 dc now and throughout), 9 dc in ring, sl st to top of ch 3 to join—10 dc.

Round 2: Ch 3, 2 dc in same st, 1 sc in next st, *5 dc in next st, 1 sc in next st; repeat from * around, 2 dc in same st as 1st 3 dc, sl st to top of ch 3 to join—25 dc + 5 sc.

Round 3: Ch 3, 2 dc in same st, 1 dc in next st, [skip 1 st, 1 dc in next st] twice, *5 dc in next st, 1 dc in next st, [skip 1 st, 1 dc in next st] twice; repeat from * around, 2 dc in same st as 1st 3 dc, sl st to top of ch 3 to join—40 dc.

Round 4: Ch 3, 2 dc in same st, 2 dc in next st, 1 dc in next st, [skip 1 st, 1 dc in next st] twice, 2 dc in next st, *5 dc in next st, 2 dc in next st, 1 dc in next st, [skip 1 st, 1 dc in next st] twice, 2 dc in next st; repeat from * around, 2 dc in same st as 1st 3 dc, sl st to top of ch 3 to join—60 dc.

Rounds 5–12: Ch 3, 2 dc in same st, 1 dc in each of the next 2 sts, [skip 1 st, 1 dc in next st] 4 times, 1 dc in next st, *5 dc in next st, 1 dc in each of the next 2 sts, [skip 1 st, 1 dc in next st] 4 times, 1 dc in next st; repeat from * around, 2 dc in same st as 1st 3 dc, sl st to top of ch 3 to join—60 dc.

Round 13: Ch 1 (does not count as a st now and throughout), skip 1st st, 1 sc in next st, 1 hdc in each of the next 2 sts, 1 dc in each of the next 2 sts, 1 tr in next st, 1 dc in each of the next 2 sts, 1 hdc in each of the next 2 sts, 1 sc in next st, *skip next st, 1 sc in next st, 1 hdc in each of the next 2 sts, 1 dc in each of the next 2 sts, 1 tr in next st, 1 dc in each of the next 2 sts, 1 hdc in each of the next 2 sts, 1 sc in next st; repeat from around, sl st to 1st sc to join—10 sc + 20 hdc + 20 dc + 5 tr.

Round 14: Ch 1, 1 sc in same st, 1 sc in each st around, sl st to 1st sc to join—55 sc.

Round 15: Ch 1, 1 sc in same st, 1 sc in each st around, invisible join to 1st sc, and fasten off—55 sc.

Twinkle Slouchy Beanie

Twinkle Slouchy Beanie

This oversized slouchy beanie makes a statement both with size and sparkle! Super bulky yarn makes it a quick project that will be extra cozy to wear.

YARN
Lion Brand Wool-Ease Thick & Quick, #6 super bulky weight yarn, acrylic/wool, 6 oz (170 g) per skein: 110 yd (101 m) of #304 Gemstone

MATERIALS
» US Size N/13 (9 mm) crochet hook or size needed to obtain gauge
» Yarn needle
» Scissors

DIFFICULTY
Easy

SIZES
One size

FINISHED MEASUREMENTS
Length: 13 in (33 cm)
Circumference: 21 in (53 cm)

GAUGE
9 dc and 4 rows = 4 in (10 cm)

NOTES
» Edging of hat is worked flat in rows and then stitched together to form a band. Body of hat is then worked in joined rounds into the side of the edging.
» Ch 3 in beginning of rounds always counts as 1 dc.

EDGING

Row 1 (RS): Ch 9 (1st 3 chs count as 1 dc), 1 dc in 4th ch from hook and in each ch across—7 dc.

Row 2: Ch 2 (counts as 1 FPdc) and turn, 1 FPdc in each st across—7 FPdc.

Row 3: Ch 2 (counts as 1 dc) and turn, 1 dc in each st across—7 dc.

Rows 4–23: Repeat rows 2–3.

Row 24: Repeat row 2.

Cut yarn, leaving a long tail. Using your yarn needle and the tail, stitch final row to beginning chain to form a band, and fasten off.

BODY OF HAT

Begin in last st of row 24, working in edge of band with RS facing you.

Round 1: Ch 3 (counts as 1 dc now and throughout), 3 dc in same st, *skip 1 st, 4 dc in next st; repeat from * around, sl st to join to top of ch 3—12 sets of 4 dc.

Rounds 2–6: Ch 3, 3 dc in same st, *skip 3 dc, 4 dc in next st; repeat from * around, sl st to join to top of ch 3—12 sets of 4 dc.

Round 7: Ch 3, 2 dc in same st, *skip 3 dc, 3 dc in next st; repeat from * around, sl st to join to top of ch 3—12 sets of 3 dc.

Round 8: Ch 3, 1 dc in same st, *skip 2 dc, 2 dc in next st; repeat from * around, sl st to join to top of ch 3—12 sets of 2 dc.

Round 9: Ch 3, *skip 1 dc, 1 dc in next st; repeat from * around, sl st to join to top of ch 3—12 dc.

Cut yarn, leaving a long tail. Using yarn needle and the tail, stitch around round 9. Pull tight to cinch shut and fasten off.

Ginger Snap Slouchy Hat

This stylish slouchy hat is packed with texture using a variety of fun stitches. A couple of buttons added to the faux flap on the side are the perfect finishing touch!

YARN

Premier Deborah Norville Everyday Soft Worsted Heathers, #4 medium worsted weight yarn, acrylic, 4 oz (113 g) per skein: 210 yd (192 m) of #14 Terracotta Heather

MATERIALS

» US Size I/9 (5.5 mm) crochet hook or size needed to obtain gauge
» Yarn needle
» Scissors
» Stitch marker
» Two 1-in (3 cm) buttons

DIFFICULTY

Intermediate

SIZES

One size

FINISHED MEASUREMENTS

Length: 11 in (28 cm)
Circumference: 21 in (53 cm)

GAUGE

14 dc and 10 rows = 6 in (15 cm)

NOTES

» Pattern is worked in joined rounds, with the exception of the band, which is worked in rows.
» Ch 1 or 2 in the beginning of rounds does not count as a st.
» Ch 3 at beginning of rounds will always count as 1 dc. Ch 4 at beginning of rounds will always count as 1 dc + 1 ch.

INSTRUCTIONS

Make a magic ring.

Round 1: Ch 3 (counts as 1 dc now and throughout), 10 dc in ring, sl st to top of 3rd ch to join—11 dc.

Round 2: Ch 4 (counts as 1 dc + 1 ch now and throughout), 1 FPdc in same st, *1 dc in next st, ch 1, 1 FPdc in same st; repeat from * around, sl st to top of 3rd ch to join—11 dc + 11 ch-1 spaces + 11 FPdc.

Round 3: Sl st into 1st ch space, ch 4, 1 dc in same ch space, 1 FPdc in next st, ch 1, 1 FPdc in same st, *1 dc in next ch space, ch 1, 1 dc in same ch space, 1 FPdc in next st, ch 1, 1 FPdc in same st; repeat from * around, sl st to top of 3rd ch to join—22 dc + 22 ch-1 spaces + 22 FPdc.

Round 4: Sl st into 1st ch space, ch 3, 1 dc in same ch space, ch 1, 1 dc in same ch space, 1 FPdc in next FPdc, ch 1, 1 FPdc in next FPdc, *2 dc in next ch space, ch 1, 1 dc in same ch space, 1 FPdc in next FPdc, ch 1, 1 FPdc in next FPdc; repeat from * around, sl st to top of 3rd ch to join—33 dc + 22 ch-1 spaces + 22 FPdc.

Round 5: Sl st into 1st ch space, ch 4, 1 dc in same ch space, 2 dc in next ch space, ch 1, 2 dc in same ch space, *1 dc in next ch space, ch 1, 1 dc in same ch space, 2 dc in next ch space, ch 1, 2 dc in same ch space; repeat from * around, sl st to top of 3rd ch to join—66 dc + 22 ch-1 spaces.

Round 6: Ch 2 (does not count as a st now and throughout), 1 FPdc in 1st dc, ch 1, 1 FPdc in next dc, 2 dc in next ch space, ch 1, 2 dc in same ch space, *1 FPdc in next dc, ch 1, 1 FPdc in next dc, 2 dc in next ch space, ch 1, 2 dc in same ch space; repeat from * around, sl st to 1st FPdc to join—44 dc + 22 ch-1 spaces + 22 FPdc.

Round 7: Ch 2 (does not count as a st now and throughout), 1 FPdc in 1st FPdc, ch 1, 1 FPdc in next FPdc, 2 dc in next ch space, ch 1, 2 dc in same ch space, *1 FPdc in next FPdc, ch 1, 1 FPdc in next FPdc, 2 dc in next ch space, ch 1, 2 dc in same ch space; repeat from * around, sl st to 1st FPdc to join—44 dc + 22 ch-1 spaces + 22 FPdc.

Round 8: Sl st into 1st ch space, ch 3, 1 dc in same ch space, ch 1, 2 dc in same ch space, 1 dc in next ch space, ch 1, 1 dc in same ch space, *2 dc in next ch space, ch 1, 2 dc in same ch space, 1 dc in next ch space, ch 1, 1 dc in same ch space; repeat from * around, sl st to top of 3rd ch to join—66 dc + 22 ch-1 spaces.

Round 9: Sl st into 1st ch space, ch 3, 1 dc in same ch space, ch 1, 2 dc in same ch space, 1 FPdc in next dc, ch 1, 1 FPdc in next dc, *2 dc in next ch space, ch 1, 2 dc in same ch space, 1 FPdc in next dc, ch 1, 1 FPdc in next dc; repeat from * around, sl st to top of 3rd ch to join—44 dc + 22 ch-1 spaces + 22 FPdc.

Round 10: Sl st into 1st ch space, ch 3, 1 dc in same ch space, ch 1, 2 dc in same ch space, 1 FPdc in next FPdc, ch 1, 1 FPdc in next FPdc, *2 dc in next ch space, ch 1, 2 dc in same ch space, 1 FPdc in next FPdc, ch 1, 1 FPdc in next FPdc; repeat from * around, sl st to top of 3rd ch to join—44 dc + 22 ch-1 spaces + 22 FPdc.

Rounds 11–16: Repeat rounds 5–10.

Rounds 17–18: Repeat rounds 5–6.

Round 19: Ch 2 (does not count as a st now and throughout), 1 FPdc in 1st FPdc, ch 1, 1 FPdc in next FPdc, 1 dc in next ch space, ch 1, 1 dc in same ch space, *1 FPdc in next FPdc, ch 1, 1 FPdc in next FPdc, 1 dc in next ch space, ch 1, 1 dc in same ch space, invisible join to 1st FPdc and fasten off—22 dc + 22 ch-1 spaces + 22 FPdc.

BAND

Count 24 sts to the left of the invisible join and place a stitch marker.

Row 1: Ch 12, 1 sc in 2nd ch from hook, 1 sc in each of the next 10 chs, join to hat by making 1 sc in st with marker (remove marker), 1 sc in each of the next 65 sts/ch spaces—77 sc.

Row 2: Ch 1 (does not count as a st now and throughout) and turn, 1 sl st in each st across—77 sl st.

Row 3: Ch 1 and turn, 1 sc in each st across—77 sc.

Rows 4–7: Repeat rows 2–3 twice.

FINISHING

Fasten off after row 7, leaving a tail. Use tail and yarn needle to stitch flap down. Attach buttons to flap.

Spring Blossom Slouchy Hat

This fun, mesh slouchy hat has a big flowery burst on the back! It's light and lacy, making it the perfect hat for spring or even summer nights.

YARN
Lion Brand Heartland, #4 medium worsted weight yarn, acrylic, 5 oz (141 g) per skein: 15 yd (14 m) of #174 Joshua Tree (**A**), 15 yd (14 m) of #158 Yellowstone (**B**), 15 yd (14 m) of #195 Biscayne (**C**), and 170 yd (155 m) of #122 Grand Canyon (**D**)

MATERIALS
» US Size I/9 (5.5 mm) crochet hook or size needed to obtain gauge
» Yarn needle
» Scissors
» Stitch marker

DIFFICULTY
Easy

SIZES
One size

FINISHED MEASUREMENTS
Length: 9 in (23 cm)
Circumference: 20 in (51 cm)

GAUGE
Work rounds 1–3. Resulting circle should measure 5 in (13 cm) across. Or 6 sc and 16 rows = 4 in (10 cm)

SPECIAL STITCHES

4 dc Bobble (bo): [Yo, insert hook into st, yo and draw up a loop, yo and draw through 2 loops] 4 times, yo and draw through all loops on hook.

Puff (pf): [Yo, insert hook into stitch, yo and pull up a loop] 3 times, yo and pull through all 7 loops on hook.

NOTES

» Rounds 1–3 and 25–28 are worked in joined rounds.

» Rounds 4–24 are worked in continuous rounds. Use a stitch marker to keep track of rounds.

With **A**, make a magic ring.

Round 1: Ch 3 (counts as 1 dc), 15 dc in ring, invisible join to top of ch 3 and fasten off **A**—16 dc.

Round 2: With **B**, (starting in any st) ch 2 (does not count as a st), 1 pf in same st, ch 2, *1 pf in next st, ch 2; repeat from * around, invisible join to 1st pf and fasten off **B**—16 pf + 16 ch-2 spaces.

Round 3: With **C**, (starting in any ch space) ch 2 (counts as first part of bo), [Yo, insert hook into same ch space, yo and draw up a loop, yo and draw through 2 loops] 3 times, yo and draw through all loops on hook (counts as 1 bo), ch 2, *1 bo in next ch sp, ch 2; repeat from * around, invisible join to 1st bo and fasten off **C**—16 bo + 16 ch-2 spaces.

Round 4: With **D**, (starting in any ch space) ch 4, 1 sc in same sp, ch 3, *1 sc in next ch space, ch 3, 1 sc in same sp, ch 3; repeat from * around, do not join—32 ch space + 32 sc.

Rounds 5–24: *1 sc in next ch space, ch 3; repeat from * around, do not join—32 ch spaces + 32 sc.

Round 25: 2 sc in each ch space, invisible join to 1st sc and fasten off **D**—64 sc.

Round 26: With **B**, 1 sc in each st, invisible join to 1st sc, and fasten off **B**—64 sc.

Round 27: With **A**, 1 sc in each st, invisible join to 1st sc, and fasten off **A**—64 sc.

Round 28: With **D**, 1 sc in each st, invisible join to 1st sc, and fasten off **D**—64 sc.

Skate Date Beanie

Skate Date Beanie

This colorblock beanie is great for using up leftover yarn. Grab three colors you like together and use this pretty textured stitch pattern to create a beanie you'll love!

YARN
Knit Picks Wool of the Andes, #4 medium worsted weight yarn, wool, 2 oz (50 g) per skein: 70 (80) yd / 64 (73) m of #24648 Green Tea Heather (**A**), 50 (60) yd / 46 (55) m of #23766 Avocado (**B**), and 60 (70) yd / 55 (64) m of #240662 Thyme (**C**)

MATERIALS
» US Size I/9 (5.5 mm) crochet hook or size needed to obtain gauge
» Yarn needle
» Scissors

DIFFICULTY
Easy

SIZES
Small (Large)

FINISHED MEASUREMENTS
Small:
    Length: 8 in (20 cm)
    Circumference: 20 in (51 cm)
Large:
    Length: 9 in (23 cm)
    Circumference: 23 in (58 cm)

GAUGE
[1 sc, 1 hdc, 1 dc] 5 times as worked in pattern and 12 rows = 4 in (10 cm)

NOTES

» Ch 1 at the beginning of rows does not count as a st.

» Pattern is worked in joined rounds and you will be turning at the beginning of each round with the exception of the final two rounds.

» Make the 1st st of each round into the st you joined to.

» Pattern is written for size Small with adjustments for size Large in parentheses.

INSTRUCTIONS

With **A**, make a magic ring.

Round 1 (RS): Ch 3 (counts as 1 dc), 11 (13) dc in ring, sl st to top of ch 3 to join—12 (14) dc.

Round 2: Ch 2 (counts as 1 hdc) and turn, 1 dc in same st, *1 hdc in next st, 1 dc in same st; repeat from * around, sl st to top of ch 2 to join—12 (14) hdc + 12 (14) dc.

Round 3: Ch 1 (does not count as a st) and turn, *1 sc in next st, [1 sc, 1 hdc] in next st; repeat from * around, sl st to 1st sc to join—24 (28) sc + 12 (14) hdc.

Round 4: Ch 1 (does not count as a st) and turn, [1 sc, 1 hdc] in each sc around, sl st to 1st sc to join—24 (28) sc + 24 (28) hdc.

Round 5: Ch 1 (does not count as a st) and turn, *[1 sc, 1 hdc, 1 dc] in next sc, [1 sc, 1 hdc] in next sc; repeat from * around, sl st to 1st sc to join—24 (28) sc + 24 (28) hdc + 12 (14) dc.

Rounds 6–11: Ch 1 (does not count as a st) and turn, [1 sc, 1 hdc, 1 dc] in each sc around, sl st to 1st sc to join—24 (28) sc + 24 (28) hdc + 24 (28) dc.

Fasten off **A** after round 11.

Rounds 12–17 (18): With **B**, repeat round 6.

Fasten off **B** after round 17 (18).

Rounds 18–23 (19–25): With **C**, repeat round 6.

Round 24 (26): Ch 1 (does not count as a st), 1 BLO sc in each st around, sl st to 1st sc to join—72 (84) sc.

Round 25 (27): Ch 1 (does not count as a st), 1 BLO sc in each st around, invisible join to 1st sc, and fasten off **C**—72 (84) sc.

Avenue C Slouchy Hat

Avenue C Slouchy Hat

This trendy slouchy hat mixes rounds of half double crochets with puff stitches to create stripes. Using a sparkly yarn for the puff stitches is sure to make it stand out!

YARN
Caron Simply Soft Party, #4 medium worsted weight yarn, acrylic/polyester, 3 oz (85 g) per skein: 140 yd (128 m) of #17 Chocolate Sparkle (**A**); Caron Simply Soft, #4 medium worsted weight yarn, acrylic, 6 oz (170 g) per skein: 120 yd (110 m) of #9783 Taupe (**B**)

MATERIALS
» US Size J/10 (6 mm) crochet hook or size needed to obtain gauge
» Yarn needle
» Scissors

DIFFICULTY
Easy

SIZES
One size

FINISHED MEASUREMENTS
Length: 10 in (25 cm)
Circumference: 20 in (51 cm)

GAUGE
12 hdc and 12 rows = 4 in (10 cm)

SPECIAL STITCHES
Puff (pf): [Yo, insert hook into stitch, yo and pull up a loop] 3 times, yo and pull through all 7 loops on hook.

NOTES

» Pattern is worked in joined rounds.
» Chs at the beginning of rounds do not count as a st.
» Carry each color up to minimize the number of cut ends.

INSTRUCTIONS

With **A**, make a magic ring.

Round 1: Ch 2 (does not count as a st now and throughout), 12 pf in ring, sl st to join to 1st pf—12 pf.

Round 2: With **B**, ch 2 (does not count as a st now and throughout), 1 hdc in same st, 2 hdc in each st around, sl st to join to 1st hdc—24 hdc.

Round 3: Ch 2, 1 hdc in same st, 2 hdc in next st, *1 hdc in next st, 2 hdc in next st; repeat from * around, sl st to join to 1st hdc—36 hdc.

Round 4: Ch 2, 1 hdc in each st around, sl st to join to 1st hdc—36 hdc.

Round 5: With **A**, ch 2, 1 pf in each st around, sl st to join to 1st pf—36 pf.

Round 6: With **B**, ch 2, 1 hdc in same st, 1 hdc in next st, 2 hdc in next st, *1 hdc in each of the next 2 sts, 2 hdc in next st; repeat from * around, sl st to join to 1st hdc—48 hdc.

Round 7: Ch 2, 1 hdc in same st, 1 hdc in each of the next 2 sts, 2 hdc in next st, *1 hdc in each of the next 3 sts, 2 hdc in next st; repeat from * around, sl st to join to 1st hdc—60 hdc.

Round 8: Ch 2, 1 hdc in each st around, sl st to join to 1st hdc—60 hdc.

Round 9: With **A**, ch 2, 1 pf in each st around, sl st to join to 1st pf—60 pf.

Round 10: With **B**, ch 2, 1 hdc in same st, 1 hdc in each of the next 3 sts, 2 hdc in next st, *1 hdc in each of the next 4 sts, 2 hdc in next st; repeat from * around, sl st to join to 1st hdc—72 hdc.

Rounds 11–12: Ch 2, 1 hdc in each st around, sl st to join to 1st hdc—72 hdc.

Round 13: With **A**, ch 2, 1 pf in each st around, sl st to join to 1st pf—72 pf.

Rounds 14–16: With **B**, ch 2, 1 hdc in each st around, sl st to join to 1st hdc—72 hdc.

Round 17: With **A**, ch 2, 1 pf in each st around, sl st to join to 1st pf—72 pf.

Rounds 18–19: With **B**, ch 2, 1 hdc in each st around, sl st to join to 1st hdc—72 hdc.

Round 20: Ch 2, 1 hdc in same st, 1 hdc in each of the next 3 sts, hdc2tog, *1 hdc in each of the next 4 sts, hdc2tog; repeat from * around, sl st to join to 1st hdc—48 hdc + 12 hdc2tog.

Round 21: With **A**, ch 2, 1 pf in each st around, sl st to join to 1st pf and fasten off **A**—60 pf.

Rounds 22–23: With **B**, ch 1 (does not count as a st now and throughout), 1 sc in each st around, sl st to join to 1st sc—60 sc.

Round 24: Ch 1, 1 sc in each st around, invisible join to 1st sc and fasten off **B**—60 sc.

Ivy Slouchy Beanie

Ivy Slouchy Beanie

This stylish slouchy beanie features ribbon woven around and just the right amount of slouch! Crossed stitches create a really unique texture but are quick and easy to crochet.

YARN
Cascade 220 Superwash, #4 medium worsted weight yarn, wool, 3.5 oz (100 g) per skein: 210 yd (192 m) of #1919 Turtle

MATERIALS
» US Size I/9 (5.5 mm) crochet hook or size needed to obtain gauge
» ¾-in (2 cm) ribbon
» Yarn needle
» Scissors

DIFFICULTY
Easy

SIZES
One size

FINISHED MEASUREMENTS
Length: 10.5 in (27 cm)
Circumference: 18 in (46 cm)

GAUGE
17 dc and 7 rows = 4 in (10 cm)

NOTES
» Pattern is worked in joined rounds, starting at the edge and working to the top.
» Hat is worked as a tube, and the top will be cinched shut at the end.
» Ch 1 at beginning of rounds does not count as a st.
» Ch 3 at beginning of rounds always counts as 1 dc.

INSTRUCTIONS

Ch 68, sl st to 1st ch to join.

Round 1: Ch 1 (does not count as a st), 1 sc in each ch around, sl st to 1st sc to join—68 sc.

Rounds 2–4: Ch 1 (does not count as a st), 1 sc in each st around, sl st to 1st sc to join—68 sc.

Round 5: Ch 4 (counts as 1 tr), 1 tr in each st around, sl st to top of ch 4 to join—68 tr.

Rounds 6–19: Ch 3 (counts as 1 dc now and throughout), 1 dc in each of the next 2 sts, 1 dc in st before ch 3, *skip 1 st, 1 dc in each of the next 3 sts, 1 dc in skipped st; repeat from * around, sl st to top of ch 3 to join—68 dc.

Round 20: Ch 3, dc2tog, 1 dc in st before ch 3, *skip 1 st, 1 dc in next st, dc2tog, 1 dc in skipped st; repeat from * around, sl st to top of ch 3 to join—34 dc + 17 dc2tog.

Round 21: Ch 3, 1 dc in next st, 1 dc in st before ch 3, *skip 1 st, dc2tog, 1 dc in skipped st; repeat from * around, sl st to top of ch 3 to join—18 dc + 16 dc2tog.

Cut yarn, leaving a long tail, and pull through st. Use yarn needle and tail to stitch around the top of the tube. Pull tight to cinch the end shut, and fasten off.

Add ribbon to round 5 by weaving ribbon under one tr and over the next, repeating all the way around. End with ends of the ribbon inside the hat, tie a knot to secure, and trim excess.

Amethyst Slouchy Hat

This lightweight slouchy hat is perfect for warmer days when you still want to be fashionable! It uses spike stitches to give the stripes a little something extra.

YARN
Red Heart Unforgettable, #4 medium worsted weight yarn, acrylic, 3.5 oz (100 g) per skein: 100 yd (91 m) of #3930 Pearly (**A**) and 100 yd (91 m) of #3950 Petunia (**B**)

MATERIALS
» US Size I/9 (5.5 mm) crochet hook or size needed to obtain gauge
» Yarn needle
» Scissors

DIFFICULTY
Easy

SIZES
One size

FINISHED MEASUREMENTS
Length: 10 in (25 cm)
Circumference: 20 in (51 cm)

GAUGE
14 dc and 7 rows = 4 in (10 cm)

SPECIAL STITCHES
Spike single crochet (ssc): Insert hook in st below next st, yo, draw up a loop to the height of the current round, yo, draw through both loops on hook.

NOTES

» Ch 3 at beginning of rounds will always count as 1 dc.
» Ch 1 at beginning of rounds will not count as a stitch.
» Carry each color up to minimize the number of cut ends.
» Dc2tog will count as 1 dc in stitch count at end of rounds.

INSTRUCTIONS

With **A**, make a magic ring.

Round 1: Ch 3 (counts as 1 dc now and throughout), 13 dc in ring, sl st to join to top of ch 3—14 dc.

Round 2: Ch 3, 1 dc in same st, 2 dc in each st around, sl st to join to top of ch 3—28 dc.

Round 3: With **B**, ch 1 (does not count as a st now and throughout), *1 sc in each of the next 3 sts, 1 ssc in next st; repeat from * around, sl st to join to 1st sc—21 sc + 7 ssc.

Round 4: Ch 3, 2 dc in next st, *1 dc in next st, 2 dc in next st; repeat from * around, sl st to join to top of ch 3—42 dc.

Round 5: Ch 3, 1 dc in next st, 2 dc in next st, *1 dc in each of the next 2 sts, 2 dc in next st; repeat from * around, sl st to join to top of ch 3—56 dc.

Round 6: With **A**, ch 1, *1 sc in each of the next 3 sts, 1 ssc in next st; repeat from * around, sl st to join to 1st sc—42 sc + 14 ssc.

Round 7: Ch 3, 1 dc in each of the next 2 sts, 2 dc in next st, *1 dc in each of the next 3 sts, 2 dc in next st; repeat from * around, sl st to join to top of ch 3—70 dc.

Round 8: Ch 3, 1 dc in each of the next 3 sts, 2 dc in next st, *1 dc in each of the next 4 sts, 2 dc in next st; repeat from * around, sl st to join to top of ch 3—84 dc.

Round 9: With **B**, ch 1, *1 sc in each of the next 3 sts, 1 ssc in next st; repeat from * around, sl st to join to 1st sc—63 sc + 21 ssc.

Rounds 10–11: Ch 3, 1 dc in each st around, sl st to join to top of ch 3—84 dc.

Round 12: With **A**, ch 1, *1 sc in each of the next 3 sts, 1 ssc in next st; repeat from * around, sl st to join to 1st sc—63 sc + 21 ssc.

Rounds 13–14: Ch 3, 1 dc in each st around, sl st to join to top of ch 3—84 dc.

Rounds 15–17: Repeat rounds 9–11.

Rounds 18–19: Repeat rounds 12–13.

Round 20: Ch 3, 1 dc in each of the next 3 sts, dc2tog, *1 dc in each of the next 4 sts, dc2tog; repeat from * around, sl st to join to top of ch 3—70 dc.

Round 21: With **B**, ch 1, *1 sc in each of the next 4 sts, 1 ssc in next st; repeat from * around, sl st to join to 1st sc—56 sc + 14 ssc.

Rounds 22–23: Ch 1, 1 BLO sc in each st around, sl st to join to 1st sc—70 BLO sc.

Round 24: Ch 1, 1 BLO sc in each st around, invisible join to 1st sc, and fasten off—70 BLO sc.

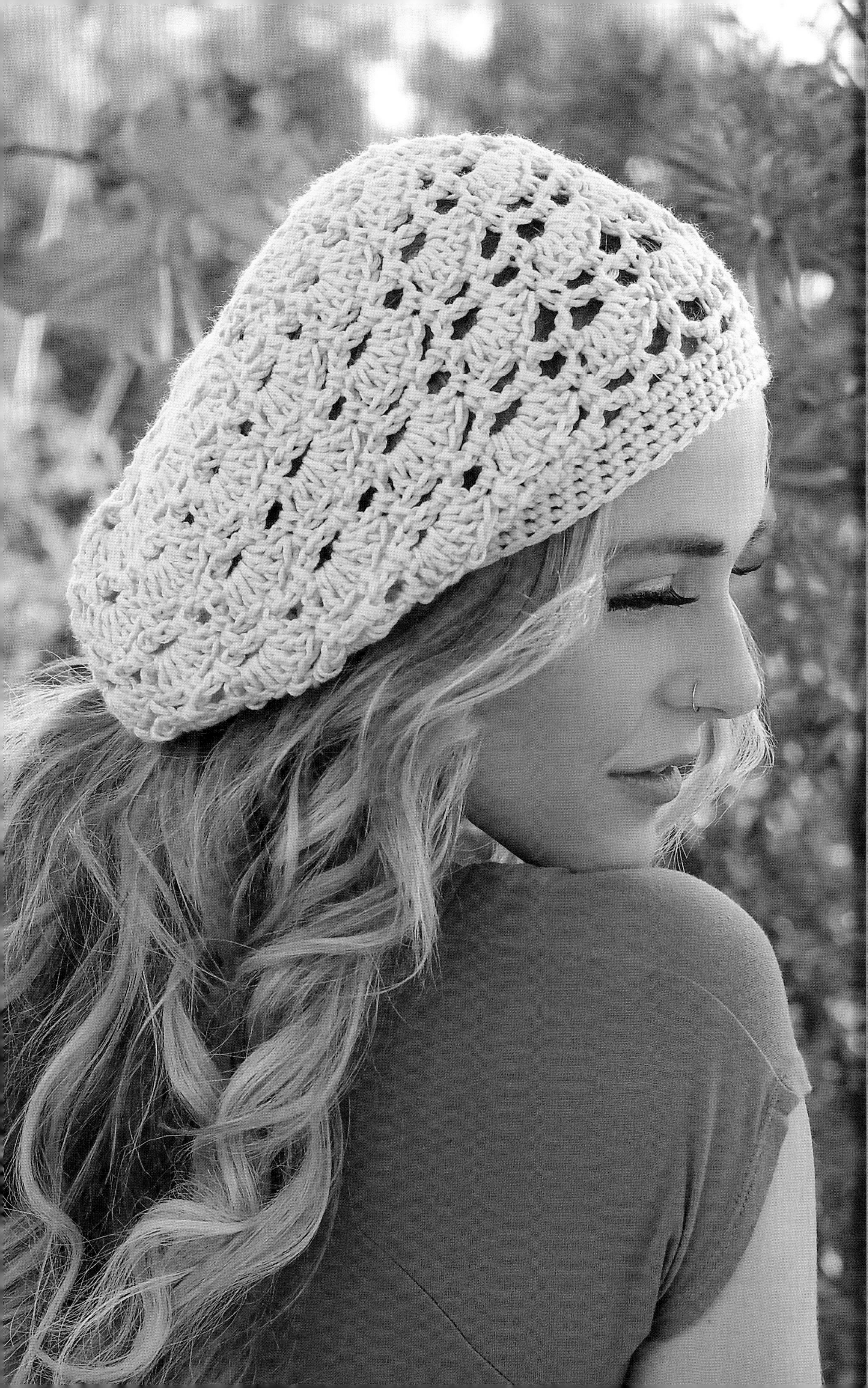

Pineapple Coconut Slouchy Hat

Pineapple Coconut Slouchy Hat

This pretty, lacy slouchy hat only requires one skein of yarn. This dainty hat looks lovely in any color and is great for spring or even summer nights!

YARN
Cascade Sateen, #4 medium worsted weight yarn, acrylic, 3.5 oz (100 g) per skein: 170 yd (155 m) of #32 Opal

MATERIALS
» US Size H/8 (5 mm) crochet hook or size needed to obtain gauge
» Yarn needle
» Scissors

DIFFICULTY
Easy

SIZES
One size

FINISHED MEASUREMENTS
Length: 10 in (25 cm)
Circumference: 20 in (51 cm)

GAUGE
16 dc and 6 rows = 4 in (10 cm)

NOTES
» Pattern is worked in rounds. Some rounds will require joining while others will not.

INSTRUCTIONS

Make a magic ring.

Round 1: Ch 3 (counts as 1 dc), 15 dc in ring, sl st to top of ch 3 to join—16 dc.

Round 2: Ch 4 (counts as 1 dc and 1 ch), 1 dc in next st, ch 1, *1 dc in next st, ch 1; repeat from * around, sl st to top of 3rd ch 3 to join—16 dc + 16 ch-1 spaces.

Round 3: Sl st into next ch space, ch 3 (counts as 1 dc), 1 dc in same ch space, 1 sc in next dc, *2 dc in next ch space, 1 sc in next dc; repeat from * around, do not join—32 dc + 16 sc.

Round 4: Skip 1 dc, sl st into next dc, ch 3, *skip 1 sc and 1 dc, 1 sc in next dc, ch 3; repeat from * around, join by making 1 sc over 1st sl st—16 sc + 16 ch-3 spaces.

Round 5: Sl st into next ch space, ch 3, 1 sc in same ch space, ch 3, *1 sc in next ch space, ch 3, 1 sc in same ch space, ch 3; repeat from * around, join by making 1 sc over 1st sl st—32 sc + 32 ch-3 spaces.

Round 6: Sl st into next ch space, 4 dc in next ch space, *1 sc in next ch space, 4 dc in next ch space; repeat from * around, join by making 1 sc over 1st sl st—64 dc + 16 sc.

Round 7: *Ch 3, skip 2 dc, 1 sc in next dc, ch 3, 1 sc in next sc; repeat from * around, do not join—32 sc + 32 ch-3 spaces.

Round 8: Sl st into next ch space, ch 3, *1 sc in next ch space, ch 3; repeat from * around, join by making 1 sc over 1st sl st—32 sc + 32 ch-3 spaces.

Round 9: Sl st into next ch space, 5 dc in next ch space, *1 sc in next ch space, 5 dc in next ch space; repeat from * around, join by making 1 sc over 1st sl st—80 dc + 16 sc.

Rounds 10–18: Repeat rounds 7–9.

Round 19: Repeat round 7.

Round 20: Sl st into next ch space, ch 2, *1 sc in next ch space, ch 2; repeat from * around, join by making 1 sc over 1st sl st—32 sc + 32 ch-2 spaces.

Round 21: Ch 1 (does not count as a st), *2 sc in next ch space; repeat from * around, sl st to 1st sc to join—64 sc.

Rounds 22–23: Ch 1 (does not count as a st), 1 sc in each st, sl st to 1st sc to join—64 sc.

Round 24: Ch 1 (does not count as a st), 1 sc in each st, invisible join to 1st sc, and fasten off—64 sc.

Heartbeat Slouchy Hat

Heartbeat Slouchy Hat

This striped slouchy hat mixes in dots of a third color, making it perfect for using up leftover yarn. Whichever colors you choose, you'll love wearing this trendy slouchy hat.

YARN
Red Heart Soft, #4 medium worsted weight yarn, acrylic, 5 oz (141 g) per skein: 100 yd (91 m) of #9010 Charcoal (**A**), 90 yd (82 m) of #9440 Light Grey Heather (**B**), and 40 yd (37 m) of #9251 Coral (**C**)

MATERIALS
» US Size H/8 (5 mm) crochet hook or size needed to obtain gauge
» Yarn needle
» Scissors

DIFFICULTY
Easy

SIZES
One size

FINISHED MEASUREMENTS
Length: 11 in (28 cm)
Circumference: 20 in (51 cm)

GAUGE
12 dc and 6 rows = 4 in (10 cm)

NOTES
» Hat is worked in joined rounds.
» The ch 1 at the beginning of rounds does not count as a st. The following ch 3 counts as 1 dc.
» Carry all colors up to minimize the number of cut ends.

INSTRUCTIONS

With **A**, make a magic ring.

Round 1: Ch 3 (counts as 1 dc now and throughout), 13 dc in ring, sl st to top of 3rd ch to join—14 dc.

Round 2: With **B**, ch 3 (counts as 1 dc now and throughout), BLO 1 dc in same st, ch 1, *BLO 2 dc in next st, ch 1; repeat from * around, sl st to top of 3rd ch to join—28 dc + 14 ch-1 spaces.

Round 3: With **C**, ch 1 (does not count as a st now and throughout), *1 sc in next ch space, ch 2; repeat from * around, sl st to 1st sc to join—14 sc + 14 ch-2 spaces.

Round 4: With **A**, ch 1 (does not count as a st now and throughout), sl st into next ch space, ch 3 (counts as 1 dc now and throughout), 2 dc in same ch space, *3 dc in next ch space; repeat from * around, sl st to top of 3rd ch to join 3—42 dc.

Round 5: With **B**, ch 3, BLO 1 dc in next st, ch 1, *BLO 2 dc in next st, ch 1, BLO 1 dc in each of the next 2 sts, ch 1; repeat from * around, BLO 2 dc in next st, ch 1, sl st to top of 3rd ch to join—56 dc + 28 ch-1 spaces.

Round 6: With **C**, ch 1, *1 sc in next ch space, ch 2; repeat from * around, sl st to 1st sc to join—28 sc + 28 ch spaces.

Round 7: With **A**, ch 1, sl st into next ch space, ch 3, 2 dc in same ch space, *3 dc in next ch space; repeat from * around, sl st to top of 3rd ch to join—84 dc.

Round 8: With **B**, ch 3, BLO 1 dc in next st, ch 1, *BLO 1 dc in each of the next 2 sts, ch 1; repeat from * around, join with sl st to top of 3rd ch to join—84 dc + 42 ch-1 spaces.

Round 9: With **C**, ch 1, *1 sc in next ch space, ch 2; repeat from * around, sl st to 1st sc to join—42 sc + 42 ch-2 spaces.

Round 10: With **A**, ch 1, sl st into next ch space, ch 3, 1 dc in same ch space, *2 dc in next ch space; repeat from * around, sl st to top of 3rd ch to join—84 dc.

Round 11: With **B**, ch 3, BLO 1 dc in next st, ch 1, *BLO 1 dc in each of the next 2 sts, ch 1; repeat from * around, sl st to top of 3rd ch to join—84 dc + 42 ch-1 spaces.

Round 12: With **C**, ch 1, *1 sc in next ch space, ch 2; repeat from * around, sl st to 1st sc to join—42 sc + 42 ch-2 spaces.

Rounds 13–18: Repeat rounds 10–12, 2 times.

Round 19: Repeat round 10.

Round 20: With **B**, ch 2 (counts as 1st part of 1 dc2tog), BLO 1 dc in next st (counts as 2nd part of same dc2tog), ch 1, *BLO dc2tog, ch 1; repeat from * around, sl st to top of 2nd ch to join, and fasten off **B**—42 dc2tog + 42 ch-1 spaces.

Round 21: With **C**, ch 1, *1 sc in next ch space, ch 1; repeat from * around, sl st to 1st sc to join and fasten off **C**—42 sc + 42 ch-1 spaces.

Round 22: With **A**, ch 1, *1 sc in next ch space, 2 sc in next ch space; repeat from * around, sl st to 1st sc to join—63 sc.

Round 23: Ch 1, BLO 1 sc in each st, sl st to 1st sc to join—63 sc.

Round 24: Ch 1, BLO 1 sc in each st, invisible join to 1st sc and fasten off **A**—63 sc.

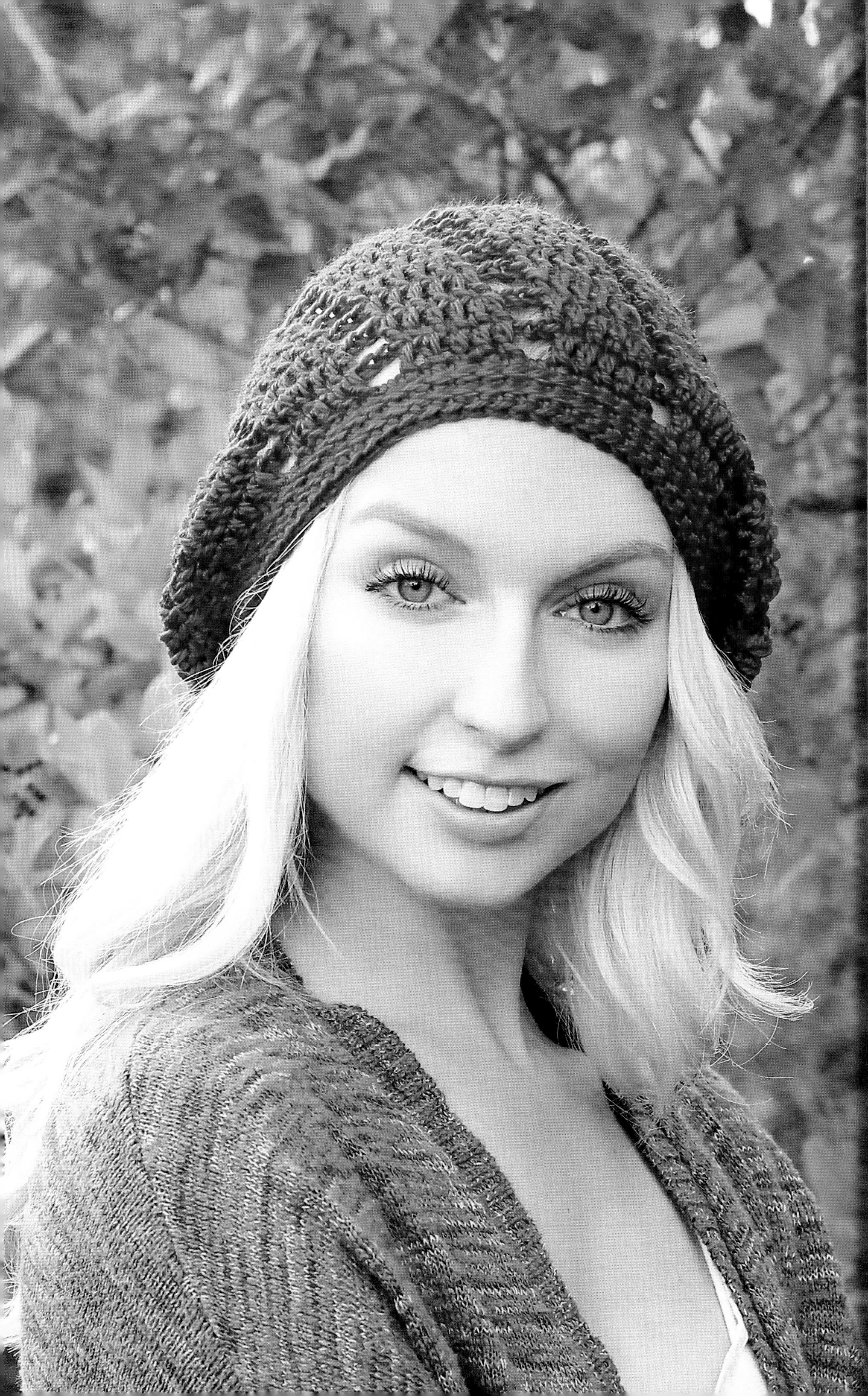

September Slouchy Hat

September Slouchy Hat

A beginner-friendly slouchy hat, September uses double crochets and chains to create a pinwheel-like pattern. Best of all, it only takes one skein of worsted weight yarn!

YARN
Yarn Bee Soft Secret, #4 medium worsted weight yarn, acrylic, 4 oz (113 g) per skein: 180 yd (165 m) of #118 Bitter Sweet

MATERIALS
» US Size I/9 (5.5 mm) crochet hook or size needed to obtain gauge
» Yarn needle
» Scissors

DIFFICULTY
Beginner

SIZES
One size

FINISHED MEASUREMENTS
Length: 10 in (25 cm)
Circumference: 20 in (51 cm)

GAUGE
16 dc and 7 rows = 4 in (10 cm)

NOTES
» Ch 3 at beginning of rounds will always count as 1 dc.
» Ch 1 at beginning of round will never count as a st.
» Pattern is worked in joined rounds with the exception of rounds 18 and 20.
» Rounds 19 and 20 will be worked into the round before the previous, in the same sts where the sl sts are worked.

INSTRUCTIONS

Make a magic ring.

Round 1: Ch 3 (counts as 1 dc now and throughout), 11 dc in ring, sl st to join to top of ch 3—12 dc.

Round 2: Ch 3, 1 dc in same st, ch 1, *2 dc in next st, ch 1; repeat from * around, sl st to join to top of ch 3—24 dc + 12 ch-1 spaces.

Round 3: Sl st in next st, ch 3, 2 dc in same st, ch 1, skip ch-1 space and next dc, *3 dc in next st, ch 1, skip ch-1 space and next dc; repeat from * around, sl st to join to top of ch 3—36 dc + 12 ch-1 spaces.

Round 4: Sl st in next st, ch 3, 1 dc in same st, 2 dc in next st, ch 2, skip ch-1 space and next dc, *2 dc in each of the next 2 sts, ch 2, skip ch-1 space and next dc; repeat from * around, sl st to join to top of ch 3—48 dc + 12 ch-2 spaces.

Round 5: Sl st in next st, ch 3, 2 dc in each of the next 2 sts, ch 2, skip ch-2 space and next dc, *1 dc in next st, 2 dc in each of the next 2 sts, ch 2, skip ch-2 space and next dc; repeat from * around, sl st to join to top of ch 3—60 dc + 12 ch-2 spaces.

Round 6: Sl st in next st, ch 3, 1 dc in next st, 2 dc in each of the next 2 sts, ch 2, skip ch-2 space and next dc, *1 dc in each of the next 2 sts, 2 dc in each of the next 2 sts, ch 2, skip ch-2 space and next dc; repeat from * around, sl st to join to top of ch 3—72 dc + 12 ch-2 spaces.

Rounds 7–15: Sl st in next st, ch 3, 1 dc in each of the next 3 sts, 2 dc in next st, ch 2, skip ch-2 space and next dc, *1 dc in each of the next 4 sts, 2 dc in next st, ch 2, skip ch-2 space and next dc; repeat from * around, sl st to join to top of ch 3—72 dc + 12 ch-2 spaces.

Round 16: Sl st in next st, ch 3, 1 dc in each of the next 4 sts, ch 1, skip ch-2 space and next dc, *1 dc in each of the next 5 sts, ch 1, skip ch-2 space and next dc; repeat from * around, sl st to join to top of ch 3—60 dc + 12 ch-1 spaces.

Round 17: Ch 1 (does not count as a st now and throughout), 1 sc in same st, 1 sc in each of the next 4 sts, 1 sc in next ch space, *1 sc in each of the next 5 sts, 1 sc in next ch space; repeat from * around, sl st to join to 1st sc—72 sc.

Round 18: 1 sl st in each st around—72 sl st.

Round 19: Sl st into 1st st of round 17, ch 1 (does not count as a st), 1 sc in each st around working into round 17, sl st to join to 1st sc—72 sc.

Round 20: Repeat round 18.

Round 21: Sl st into 1st st of round 19, ch 1 (does not count as a st), 1 sc in each st around working into round 19, invisible join to 1st sc, and fasten off—72 sc.

Cottontail Beanie

This easy one-skein beanie uses clusters of single crochets to create a pretty but subtle texture. A furry pom-pom on top is the perfect finishing touch!

YARN
Premier Deborah Norville Everyday Soft Worsted, #4 medium worsted weight yarn, acrylic, 4 oz (113 g) per skein: 160 (180) yd / 146 (166) m of #52 Chinchilla

MATERIALS
» US Size I/9 (5.5 mm) crochet hook or size needed to obtain gauge
» Yarn needle
» Scissors
» Stitch marker
» Faux fur pom-pom

DIFFICULTY
Beginner

SIZES
Small (Large)

FINISHED MEASUREMENTS
Small:
Length: 8 in (20 cm)
Circumference: 20 in (51 cm)
Large:
Length: 9 in (23 cm)
Circumference: 22 in (56 cm)

GAUGE
15 sc and 15 rows of pattern = 4 in (10 cm)

NOTES

» Hat is worked from the edge up to the top.
» Pattern is worked in continuous rounds.
» Use a stitch marker to keep track of the beginning of the round.
» Pattern is written for size Small with adjustments for size Large in parentheses.

INSTRUCTIONS

Ch 78 (84), sl st to join to 1st ch.

Round 1: Ch 1 (does not count as a st), 1 sc in each ch around—78 (84) sc.

Rounds 2–18 (2–21): *3 sc in next st, skip 2 sts; repeat from * around—78 (84) sc.

Round 19 (22): *3 sc in next st, skip 2 sts, 2 sc in next st, skip 2 sts; repeat from * around—65 (70) sc.

Round 20 (23): *3 sc in next st, skip 2 sts, 2 sc in next st, skip 1 st; repeat from * around—65 (70) sc.

Round 21 (24): *2 sc in next st, skip 2 sts, 2 sc in next st, skip 1 st; repeat from * around—52 (56) sc.

Round 22 (25): *2 sc in next st, skip 1 st; repeat from * around—52 (56) sc.

Round 23 (26): *2 sc in next st, skip 1 st, 1 sc in next st, skip 1 st; repeat from * around—39 (42) sc.

Round 24 (27): *2 sc in next st, skip 1 st, 1 sc in next st; repeat from * around—39 (42) sc.

Round 25 (28): *1 sc in next st, skip 1 st, 1 sc in next st; repeat from * around—26 (28) sc.

Round 26 (29): 1 sc in each st around—26 (28) sc.

Round 27 (30): *1 sc in next st, skip 1 st; repeat from * around—13 (14) sc.

Round 28 (small): *1 sc in next st, skip 1 st; repeat from * around, 1 sc in last st—7 sc.

Round 31 (large): *1 sc in next st, skip 1 st; repeat from * around—7 sc.

Cut yarn, leaving a tail. Use yarn needle and tail to cinch hole shut, and fasten off. Attach a faux fur pom-pom to top of hat if desired.

Festival Slouchy Hat

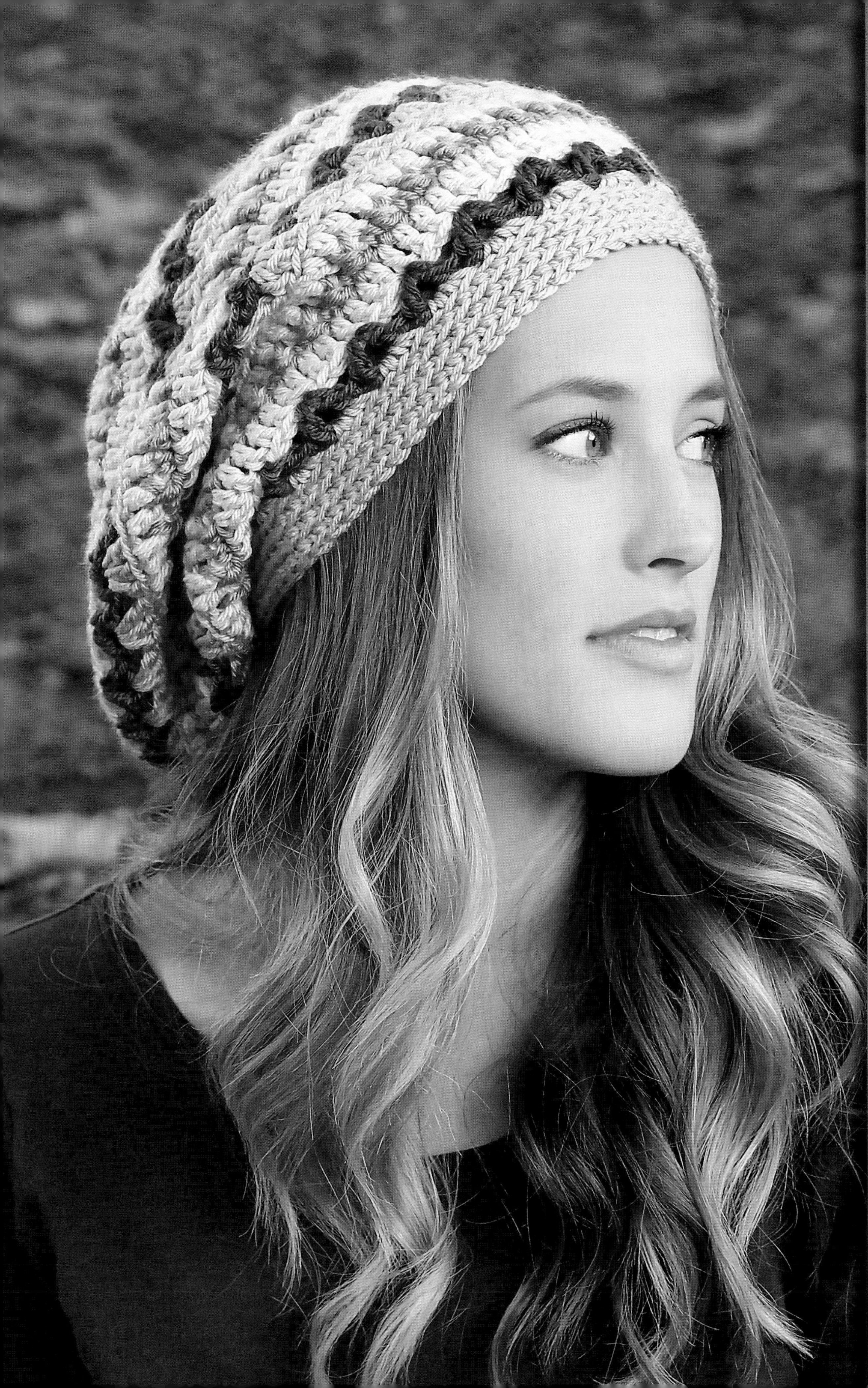

Festival Slouchy Hat

This slouchy hat uses a variety of stitches and colors for an exciting look. You'll love mixing and matching colors to create your own unique version.

YARN
Loops & Threads Colorwheel, #4 medium worsted weight yarn, acrylic, 1.75 oz (50 g) per skein: 65 yd (59 m) of #41 Toast (**A**), 85 yd (78 m) of #47 Pale Taupe (**B**), 40 yd (37 m) of #43 Eggplant (**C**), and 40 yd (37 m) of #42 Mauve (**D**)

MATERIALS
» US Size I/9 (5.5 mm) crochet hook or size needed to obtain gauge
» Yarn needle
» Scissors

DIFFICULTY
Easy

SIZES
One size

FINISHED MEASUREMENTS
Length: 11.5 in (29 cm)
Circumference: 20 in (51 cm)

GAUGE
13 dc and 6 rows = 4 in (10 cm)

NOTES
» Pattern is worked in joined rounds. Do not fasten off color at the end of rounds. Carry all colors up to minimize the number of cut ends.
» Ch 3 will always count as 1 dc.
» Ch 4 will always count as 1 dc + 1 ch.
» Ch 1 does not count as a st.

INSTRUCTIONS

With **A**, make a magic ring.

Round 1: Ch 3 (counts as 1 dc now and throughout), 13 dc in ring, sl st to top of ch 3 to join—14 dc.

Round 2: With **B**, ch 3, 1 BLO dc in same st, 2 BLO dc in each st around, sl st to top of ch 3 to join—28 BLO dc.

Round 3: With **C**, ch 4 (counts as 1 dc + 1 ch now and throughout), 1 dc in same st, *skip 1 st, 1 dc in next st, ch 1, 1 dc in same st; repeat from * around, sl st to 3rd ch to join—28 dc + 14 ch-1 spaces.

Round 4: With **A**, sl st into ch space, ch 3, 3 dc in same ch space, 4 dc in each ch space around, sl st to top of ch 3 to join—56 dc.

Round 5: With **B**, ch 3, 1 BLO dc in each of the next 2 sts, 2 BLO dc in next st, *1 BLO dc in each of the next 3 sts, 2 BLO dc in next st; repeat from * around, sl st to top of ch 3 to join—70 BLO dc.

Round 6: With **D**, ch 1 (does not count as a st now and throughout), 1 sc in same st, 1 FPdc in next st, *1 sc in next st, 1 FPdc in next st; repeat from * around, sl st to 1st sc to join—35 sc + 35 FPdc.

Round 7: With **B**, ch 3, 1 dc in each of the next 3 sts, 2 dc in next st, *1 dc in each of the next 4 sts, 2 dc in next st; repeat from * around; sl st to top of ch 3 to join—84 dc.

Round 8: With **C**, ch 4, 1 dc in same st, *skip 2 sts, 1 dc in next st, ch 1, 1 dc in same st; repeat from * around, sl st to 3rd ch to join—56 dc + 28 ch-1 spaces.

Round 9: With **A**, sl st into ch space, ch 3, 2 dc in same ch space, 3 dc in each ch space around, sl st to top of ch 3 to join—84 dc.

Round 10: With **B**, ch 3, 1 BLO dc in each st around, sl st to top of ch 3 to join—84 BLO dc.

Round 11: With **D**, ch 1, 1 sc in same st, 1 FPdc in next st, *1 sc in next st, 1 FPdc in next st; repeat from * around, sl st to 1st sc to join—42 sc + 42 FPdc.

Round 12: With **B**, ch 3, 1 dc in each st around, sl st to top of ch 3 to join—84 dc.

Rounds 13–16: Repeat rounds 8–11 once. Fasten off **D** after round 16.

Round 17: With **B**, ch 3, dc2tog, 1 dc in next st, dc2tog, *1 dc in each of the next 4 sts, dc2tog; repeat from * around, sl st to top of ch 3 to join and fasten off **B**—69 dc.

Round 18: With **C**, ch 4, 1 dc in same st, *skip 2 sts, 1 dc in next st, ch 1, 1 dc in same st; repeat from * around, sl st to 3rd ch to join and fasten off **C**—46 dc + 23 ch-1 spaces.

Round 19: With **A**, sl st into ch space, ch 1, 3 sc in same ch space, 3 sc in each ch space around, sl st to 1st sc to join—69 sc.

Rounds 20–21: With **A**, ch 1, 1 BLO sc in each st around, sl st to 1st sc to join—69 BLO sc.

Round 22: With **A**, ch 1, 1 BLO sc in each st around, invisible join to 1st sc, and fasten off **A**—69 BLO sc.

Alaska Beanie

This super cozy beanie has earflaps with long ties for extra warmth on cold days. Front post stitches create a unique texture, and tassels are a fun finishing touch!

YARN
Bernat Roving, #5 bulky weight yarn, acrylic/wool, 3.5 oz (100 g) per skein: 85 yd (78 m) of #32 Putty (**A**) and 70 yd (64 m) of #71 Plum (**B**)

MATERIALS
» US Size N/13 (9 mm) crochet hook or size needed to obtain gauge
» Yarn needle
» Scissors

DIFFICULTY
Intermediate

SIZES
One size

FINISHED MEASUREMENTS
Length: 9.5 in (24 cm) plus earflap
Circumference: 24 in (61 cm)

GAUGE
8 dc and 4 rows = 4 in (10 cm)

NOTES
» Pattern is worked in joined rounds.
» Ch 3 at beginning of rounds will count as 1 dc or FPdc as noted.
» Ch 1 at beginning of rounds does not count as a stitch.
» This yarn works up like a #6 super bulky weight. Other #5's will probably not work for this pattern.

INSTRUCTIONS

With **A**, make a magic ring.

Round 1: Ch 3 (counts as 1 dc), 10 dc in ring, sl st to top of ch 3 to join—11 dc.

Round 2: Ch 3 (counts as 1 FPdc), 1 FPdc in same st, 2 FPdc in each st around, sl st to top of ch 3 to join—22 FPdc.

Round 3: Ch 3 (counts as 1 dc), 2 dc in next st, *1 dc in next st, 2 dc in next st; repeat from * around, sl st to top of ch 3 to join—33 dc.

Round 4: Ch 3 (counts as 1 FPdc), 1 FPdc in same st, skip 1 st, 2 FPdc in next st, *2 FPdc in next st, skip 1 st, 2 FPdc in next st; repeat from * around, sl st to top of ch 3 to join—44 FPdc.

Round 5: Ch 3 (counts as 1 dc), 1 dc in each st around, sl st to top of ch 3 to join—44 dc.

Round 6: Ch 3 (counts as 1 FPdc), 1 FPdc in same st, skip 1 st, *2 FPdc in next st, skip 1 st; repeat from * around, sl st to top of ch 3 to join—44 FPdc.

Rounds 7–8: Repeat rounds 5–6, fasten off **A**.

Rounds 9–10: With **B**, repeat rounds 5–6.

Round 11: Ch 1 (does not count as a st), 1 sc in each of the next 7 sts, 1 dc in next st, 2 dc in next st, 3 tr in next st, 2 tr in next st, 2 dc in next st, 1 dc in next st, 1 sc in each of the next 18 sts, 1 dc in next st, 2 dc in next st, 2 tr in next st, 3 tr in next st, 2 dc in next st, 1 dc in next st, 1 sc in each of the next 7 sts, sl st to 1st sc to join—32 sc + 12 dc + 10 tr.

Round 12: Ch 1 (does not count as a st), 1 sc in each of the next 8 sts, 2 FPdc in next st, [skip 1 st, 2 FPdc in next st] twice, 1 dc in next st, ch 26, 1 sc in 2nd ch from hook and in each of the next 24 chs, 1 dc in same st as previous dc, 2 FPdc in next st, skip 1 st, 2 FPdc in next st, 1 sc in each of the next 20 sts, 2 FPdc in next st, skip 1 st, 2 FPdc in next st, 1 dc in next st, ch 26, 1 sc in 2nd ch from hook and in each of the next 24 chs, 1 dc in same st as previous dc, 2 FPdc in next st, [skip 1 st, 2 FPdc in next st] twice, 1 sc in each of the next 8 sts, invisible join to 1st sc, and fasten off **B**—86 sc + 20 FPdc + 4 dc.

FINISHING

Attach tassels or pom-poms to the ends of the ties if desired.

High Tide Beanie

This beanie is warm but not too heavy and is fun and easy to stitch up. Using two colors of worsted weight yarn will create vertical stripes of pretty shell stitches.

YARN
Cascade 220, #4 medium worsted weight yarn, wool, 3.5 oz (100 g) per skein: 70 yd (64 m) of #9076 Mint (**A**) and 75 yd (69 m) of #7812 Lagoon (**B**)

MATERIALS
» US Size I/9 (5.5 mm) crochet hook or size needed to obtain gauge
» Yarn needle
» Scissors

DIFFICULTY
Easy

SIZES
One size

FINISHED MEASUREMENTS
Length: 8 in (20 cm)
Circumference: 20 in (51 cm)

GAUGE
[5 dc in next sc, skip 2 dc, 1 sc in next dc, skip 2 dc] 3 times and 9 rows = 5 in (13 cm)

NOTES
» Pattern is worked in joined rounds.
» Ch 1 at beginning of rounds never counts as a stitch.
» Ch 3 at beginning of rounds always counts as 1 dc.

With **A**, make a magic ring.

Round 1: Ch 3 (counts as 1 dc now and throughout), 21 dc in ring, sl st to top of ch 3 to join—22 dc.

Round 2: With **B**, ch 1 (does not count as a st now and throughout), 1 sc in same st, 2 dc in next st, *1 sc in next st, 2 dc in next st; repeat from * around, sl st to 1st sc to join—22 dc + 11 sc.

Round 3: With **A**, ch 3, 1 dc in same st, skip 1 dc, 1 sc in next dc, *3 dc in next sc, skip 1 dc, 1 sc in next dc; repeat from * around, 1 dc in same st as 1st dc, sl st to top of ch 3 to join—33 dc + 11 sc.

Round 4: With **B**, ch 1, 1 sc in same st, skip 1 dc, 4 dc in next sc, skip 1 dc, *1 sc in next dc, skip 1 dc, 4 dc in next sc, skip 1 dc; repeat from * around, sl st to 1st sc to join—44 dc + 11 sc.

Round 5: With **A**, ch 3, 2 dc in same st, skip 2 dc, 1 sc in next dc, skip 1 dc, *5 dc in next sc, skip 2 dc, 1 sc in next dc, skip 1 dc; repeat from * around, 2 dc in same st as 1st dc, sl st to top of ch 3 to join—55 dc + 11 sc.

Round 6: With **B**, ch 1, 1 sc in same st, skip 2 dc, 5 dc in next sc, skip 2 dc, *1 sc in next dc, skip 2 dc, 5 dc in next sc, skip 2 dc; repeat from * around, sl st to 1st sc to join—55 dc + 11 sc.

Round 7: With **A**, ch 3, 2 dc in same st, skip 2 dc, 1 sc in next dc, skip 2 dc, *5 dc in next sc, skip 2 dc, 1 sc in next dc, skip 2 dc; repeat from * around, 2 dc in same st as 1st dc, sl st to top of ch 3 to join—55 dc + 11 sc.

Rounds 8–15: Repeat rounds 6–7, 4 times.

Round 16: With **B**, ch 1 and fasten off **A**, 1 sc in same st, 1 sc in each of the next 2 sts, 1 hdc in next st, *1 sc in each of the next 5 sts, 1 hdc in next st; repeat from * around, 1 sc in each of the last 2 sts, sl st to 1st sc to join—55 sc + 11 hdc.

Round 17: Ch 1, 1 sc in same st, 1 sc in each st around, sl st to 1st sc to join—66 sc.

Round 18: Ch 1, 1 sc in same st, 1 sc in each st around, invisible join to 1st sc, and fasten off **B**—66 sc.

Dew Drop Slouchy Hat

Dew Drop Slouchy Hat

A classic slouchy hat can be whipped up quickly using super bulky yarn. It's so easy, you'll want to make one to match every outfit!

YARN
Loops and Threads Cozy Wool, #6 super bulky weight yarn, wool/acrylic, 4.5 oz (127 g) per skein: 150 yd (137 m) of #10 Velvet

MATERIALS
» US Size N/13 (9 mm) crochet hook or size needed to obtain gauge
» Yarn needle
» Scissors

DIFFICULTY
Beginner

SIZES
One size

FINISHED MEASUREMENTS
Length: 10 in (25 cm)
Circumference: 20 in (51 cm)

GAUGE
8 BLO dc and 4 rows = 4 in (10 cm)

NOTES
» Ch 3 at beginning of rounds counts as 1 dc.
» Ch 1 at beginning of rounds counts as 1 sc.
» Pattern is worked in joined rounds.
» Dc2tog will count as 1 dc in stitch count.
» Sc2tog will count as 1 sc in stitch count.

INSTRUCTIONS

Make a magic ring.

Round 1: Ch 3 (counts as 1 dc now and throughout), 13 dc in ring, sl st to join to top of 3rd ch—14 dc.

Round 2: Ch 3, 1 BLO dc in same st, 2 BLO dc in each st around, sl st to join to top of 3rd ch—28 dc.

Round 3: Ch 3, 2 BLO dc in next st, *1 BLO dc in next st, 2 BLO dc in next st; repeat from * around, sl st to join to top of 3rd ch—42 dc.

Round 4: Ch 3, 1 BLO dc in next st, 2 BLO dc in next st, *1 BLO dc in each of the next 2 sts, 2 BLO dc in next st; repeat from * around, sl st to join to top of 3rd ch—56 dc.

Rounds 5–8: Ch 3, 1 BLO dc in each st around, sl st to join to top of 3rd ch—56 dc.

Round 9: Ch 3, 1 BLO dc in next st, 1 BLO dc2tog, *1 BLO dc in each of the next 2 sts, 1 BLO dc2tog; repeat from * around, sl st to join to top of 3rd ch—42 dc.

Round 10: Ch 1 (counts as 1 sc now and throughout), 1 BLO sc in each of the next 3 sts, 1 BLO sc2tog, *1 BLO sc in each of the next 4 sts, 1 BLO sc2tog; repeat from * around, sl st to join to ch 1—35 sc.

Round 11: Ch 1, 1 BLO sc in each st around, sl st to join to ch 1—35 sc.

Round 12: Ch 1, 1 BLO sc in each st around, invisible join to ch 1, and fasten off—35 sc.

Ziggy Beanie

This beanie has a slightly open but not too airy stitch pattern that is great for cool days. Alternating colors each round creates a fun zigzag design.

YARN
Cascade 220, #4 medium worsted weight yarn, wool, 3.5 oz (100 g) per skein: 90 yd (82 m) of #2441 River Rock (**A**) and 40 yd (37 m) of #7804 Shrimp (**B**)

MATERIALS
» US Size I/9 (5.5 mm) crochet hook or size needed to obtain gauge
» Yarn needle
» Scissors

DIFFICULTY
Easy

SIZES
One size

FINISHED MEASUREMENTS
Length: 8 in (20 cm)
Circumference: 20 in (51 cm)

GAUGE
[1 dc, ch 1, 1 dc] in 1 ch space 4 times and 7 rows = 4 in (10 cm)

NOTES
» Pattern is worked in joined rounds.
» Ch 3 in beginning of rounds always counts as 1 dc.
» Ch 4 in beginning of rounds always counts as 1 dc + 1 ch.

INSTRUCTIONS

With **A**, make a magic ring.

Round 1: Ch 3 (counts as 1 dc now and throughout), 11 dc in ring, sl st to top of ch 3 to join—12 dc.

Round 2: Ch 4 (counts as 1 dc + 1 ch now and throughout), 1 dc in same st, *1 dc in next st, ch 1, 1 dc in same st; repeat from * around, sl st to 3rd ch to join—24 dc + 12 ch-1 spaces.

Round 3: Sl st into next ch space, ch 4, 1 dc in same ch space, ch 1, 1 dc in same ch space, *1 dc in next ch space, [ch 1, 1 dc in same ch space] twice; repeat from * around, sl st to 3rd ch to join—36 dc + 24 ch-1 spaces.

Rounds 4–5: Sl st into next ch space, ch 4, 1 dc in same ch space, *1 dc in next ch space, ch 1, 1 dc in same ch space; repeat from * around, sl st to 3rd ch to join—48 dc + 24 ch-1 spaces.

Fasten off **A** after round 5.

Round 6: With **B**, sl st into next ch space, ch 4, 1 dc in same ch space, *1 dc in next ch space, ch 1, 1 dc in same ch space; repeat from * around, sl st to 3rd ch to join, fasten off **B**—48 dc + 24 ch-1 spaces.

Round 7: With **A**, sl st into next ch space, ch 4, 1 dc in same ch space, *1 dc in next ch space, ch 1, 1 dc in same ch space; repeat from * around, sl st to 3rd ch to join, fasten off **A**—48 dc + 24 ch-1 spaces.

Rounds 8–11: Repeat rounds 6–7 twice.

Round 12: Repeat round 6.

Round 13: With **A**, sl st into next ch space, ch 3, 2 dc in same ch space, 3 dc in each ch space around, sl st to top of ch 3 to join—72 dc.

Round 14: Ch 3, 1 FPdc in next st, *1 dc in next st, 1 FPdc in next st; repeat from * around, sl st to top of ch 3 to join—36 dc + 36 FPdc.

Round 15: Ch 3, 1 FPdc in next st, *1 dc in next st, 1 FPdc in next st; repeat from * around, invisible join to top of ch 3, and fasten off **A**—36 dc + 36 FPdc.

Pinecone Slouchy Hat

Pinecone Slouchy Hat

This cozy slouchy hat uses bobble stitches to create a pretty pinecone-like texture. Ribbon woven through the stitches gives it an extra-special finishing touch.

YARN

Lion Brand Heartland, #4 medium worsted weight yarn, acrylic, 5 oz (141 g) per skein: 270 yd (247 m) of #125 Mammoth Cave

MATERIALS

» US Size J/10 (6 mm) crochet hook or size needed to obtain gauge
» ¾-in (2 cm) ribbon
» Yarn needle
» Scissors

DIFFICULTY

Intermediate

SIZES

One size

FINISHED MEASUREMENTS

Length: 10 in (25 cm)
Circumference: 20 in (51 cm)

GAUGE

[bo, ch 1] 4 times and 5 rows = 4 in (10 cm)

SPECIAL STITCHES

5 dc Bobble (bo): [Yo, insert hook into st, yo and draw up a loop, yo and draw through 2 loops] 5 times, yo and draw through all loops on hook.

Beginning Bobble (BegBo): Ch 2 (counts as first part of bo), [yo, insert hook into same ch space, yo and draw up a loop, yo and draw through 2 loops] 4 times, yo and draw through all loops on hook.

NOTES
>> Pattern is worked in joined rounds.
>> Beginning bobble (BegBo) will count as 1 bo in stitch count at end of rounds.

Make a magic ring.

Round 1: BegBo in ring, ch 2, [1 bo in ring, ch 2] 4 times, sl st to BegBo to join—5 bo + 5 ch-2 spaces.

Round 2: Sl st into next ch space, BegBo in same ch space, ch 2, 1 bo in same ch space, ch 2. *1 bo in next ch space, ch 2, 1 bo in same ch space, ch 2; repeat from * around, sl st to BegBo to join—10 bo + 10 ch-2 spaces.

Round 3: Sl st into next ch space, BegBo in same ch space, ch 2, 1 bo in same ch space, ch 2, 1 bo in next ch space, ch 2, *1 bo in next ch space, ch 2, 1 bo in same ch space, ch 2, 1 bo in next ch space, ch 2; repeat from * around, sl st to BegBo to join—15 bo + 15 ch-2 spaces.

Round 4: Sl st into next ch space, BegBo in same ch space, ch 2, 1 bo in same ch space, ch 2, [1 bo in next ch space, ch 2] 2 times, *1 bo in next ch space, ch 2, 1 bo in same ch space, ch 2, [1 bo in next ch space, ch 2] 2 times; repeat from * around, sl st to BegBo to join—20 bo + 20 ch-2 spaces.

Round 5: Sl st into next ch space, BegBo in same ch space, ch 2, 1 bo in same ch space, ch 2, [1 bo in next ch space, ch 2] 3 times, *1 bo in next ch space, ch 2, 1 bo in same ch space, ch 2, [1 bo in next ch space, ch 2] 3 times; repeat from * around, sl st to BegBo to join—25 bo + 25 ch-2 spaces.

Rounds 6–11: Sl st into next ch space, BegBo in same ch space, ch 2, *1 bo in next ch space, ch 2; repeat from * around, sl st to BegBo to join—25 bo + 25 ch-2 spaces.

Round 12: Sl st into next ch space, BegBo in same ch space, ch 1, *1 bo in next ch space, ch 1; repeat from * around, sl st to BegBo to join—25 bo + 25 ch-1 spaces.

Round 13: Ch 4 (counts as 1 tr), 1 tr in next ch space, *1 tr in next st, 1 tr in next ch space; repeat from * around, sl st to join to top of ch 4—50 tr.

Rounds 14–16: Ch 1 (does not count as a st), 1 sc in each st around, sl st to 1st sc to join—50 sc.

Round 17: Ch 1 (does not count as a st), 1 sc in each st around, invisible join to 1st sc, and fasten off—50 sc.

Add ribbon to round 13 by weaving ribbon under one tr and over the next, repeating all the way around. End with ends of the ribbon inside the hat, tie a knot to secure, and trim excess.

Painted Desert Slouchy Beanie

Painted Desert Slouchy Beanie

This slouchy beanie uses a multicolored yarn paired with a solid color to create vertical stripes. Have fun choosing color combinations to make this comfy slouchy beanie!

YARN
Lion Brand Landscapes, #4 medium worsted weight yarn, acrylic, 3.5 oz (100 g) per skein: 125 (140) yd / 114 (128) m of #135 Rust (**A**) and 120 (135) yd /110 (123) m of #204 Desert Spring (**B**)

MATERIALS
» US Size I/9 (5.5 mm) crochet hook or size needed to obtain gauge
» Yarn needle
» Scissors

DIFFICULTY
Easy

SIZES
Small (Large)

FINISHED MEASUREMENTS
Small:
    Length: 10 in (25 cm)
    Circumference: 22 in (56 cm)
Large:
    Length: 11 in (28 cm)
    Circumference: 23 in (58 cm)

GAUGE
14 hdc and 6 rows = 4 in (10 cm)

NOTES

» Hat is worked flat in rows and then stitched together to form a tube. Top will be cinched shut. Edging is added last and is worked in a joined round.

» Change colors on every other row as instructed. Carry unused color up the side.

» Pattern is written for size Small with adjustments for size Large in parentheses.

INSTRUCTIONS

Row 1: With **A**, ch 37 (42), 1 hdc in 3rd ch from hook (1st 2 chs count as 1 hdc), 1 hdc in each remaining ch, turn—36 (41) hdc.

Row 2: With **B**, ch 1 (does not count as a st now and throughout), FLO sl st in each st across, turn—36 (41) sl st.

Row 3: Ch 3 (counts as 1 hdc now and throughout), FLO hdc in each st across, turn—36 (41) hdc.

Row 4: With **A**, ch 1 (does not count as a st now and throughout), FLO sl st in each st across, turn—36 (41) sl st.

Row 5: Ch 3 (counts as 1 hdc now and throughout), FLO hdc in each st across, turn—36 (41) hdc.

Rows 6–53 (–57): Repeat rows 2–5, 12 (13) times.

Rows 54–56 (58–60): Repeat rows 2–4 once, fasten off **A** and **B** after final rows.

Using yarn needle and a piece of **A**, stitch final row to beginning chain to form a tube and fasten off.

Using yarn needle and a piece of **A**, stitch around either end of the tube. Pull tight to cinch the end shut, and fasten off.

EDGING

With **A**, work 84 (90) sc evenly around, invisible join to first sc, and fasten off **A**—84 (90) sc.

Dandelion Slouchy Hat

Dandelion Slouchy Hat

This heavy slouchy hat uses a pretty combination of stitches along with a bulky yarn to create a hat you'll love wearing. It's so fashionable, you'll want to make one in every color.

YARN
Knit Picks Billow, #5 bulky weight yarn, pima cotton, 3.5 oz (100 g) per skein: 190 yd (174 m) of #37 Turmeric

MATERIALS
» US Size K/10.5 (6.5 mm) crochet hook or size needed to obtain gauge
» Yarn needle
» Scissors

DIFFICULTY
Easy

SIZES
One size

FINISHED MEASUREMENTS
Length: 11 in (28 cm)
Circumference: 21 in (53 cm)

GAUGE
10 hdc and 6 rows = 4 in (10 cm)

SPECIAL STITCHES
Puff stitch (pf): [Yo, insert hook into st, yo and draw up a look] 3 times, yo and draw through all 7 loops on hook.

NOTES

» Hat is worked in joined rounds with the exception of rounds 16 and 18.
» Ch 1 at beginning of rounds does not count as a st.
» Ch 2 at beginning of rounds will always count as 1 hdc.
» A hdc2tog will count as 1 hdc in stitch count at end of rounds.

INSTRUCTIONS

Make a magic ring.

Round 1: Ch 1 (does not count as a st now and throughout), [1 pf in ring, ch 1] 8 times, sl st to join to 1st pf—8 pf + 8 ch-1 spaces.

Round 2: Sl st into next ch space, ch 1, [1 pf in same ch space, ch 1] 2 times, *1 pf in next ch space, ch 1, 1 pf in same ch space, ch 1; repeat from * around, sl st to join to 1st pf—16 pf + 16 ch-1 spaces.

Round 3: Sl st into next ch space, ch 2 (counts as 1 hdc now and throughout), 2 hdc in same ch space, ch 1, 1 pf in next ch space, ch 1, *3 hdc in next ch space, ch 1, 1 pf in next ch space, ch 1; repeat from * around, sl st to join to top of ch 2—24 hdc + 8 pf + 16 ch-1 spaces.

Round 4: Ch 2, 1 hdc in next st, 2 hdc in next st, 1 pf in next ch space, ch 1, 1 pf in next ch space, *1 hdc in each of the next 2 sts, 2 hdc in next st, 1 pf in next ch space, ch 1, 1 pf in next ch space; repeat from * around, sl st to join to top of ch 2—32 hdc + 16 pf + 8 ch-1 spaces.

Round 5: Ch 2, 1 hdc in each of the next 2 sts, 2 hdc in next st, ch 1, 1 pf in next ch space, ch 1, *1 hdc in each of the next 3 sts, 2 hdc in next st, ch 1, 1 pf in next ch space, ch 1; repeat from * around, sl st to join to top of ch 2—40 hdc + 8 pf + 16 ch-1 spaces.

Round 6: Ch 2, 1 hdc in each of the next 4 sts, 1 pf in next ch space, ch 1, *1 hdc in each of the next 5 sts, 1 pf in next ch space, ch 1, 1 pf in next ch space; repeat from * around, sl st to join to top of ch 2—40 hdc + 16 pf + 8 ch-1 spaces.

Round 7: Ch 2, 1 hdc in each of the next 4 sts, ch 1, 1 pf in next ch space, ch 1, *1 hdc in each of the next 5 sts, ch 1, 1 pf in next ch space, ch 1; repeat from * around, sl st to join to top of ch 2—40 hdc + 8 pf + 16 ch-1 spaces.

Rounds 8–11: Repeat rounds 6–7.

Round 12: Repeat round 6.

Round 13: Ch 2, 1 hdc in each of the next 2 sts, hdc2tog, ch 1, 1 pf in next ch space, ch 1, *1 hdc in each of the next 3 sts, hdc2tog, ch 1, 1 pf in next ch space, ch 1; repeat from * around, sl st to join to top of ch 2—32 hdc + 8 pf + 16 ch-1 spaces.

Round 14: Ch 2, 1 hdc in next st, hdc2tog, 1 pf in next ch space, ch 1, 1 pf in next ch space, *1 hdc in each of the next 2 sts, hdc2tog, 1 pf in next ch space, ch 1, 1 pf in next ch space; repeat from * around, sl st to join to top of ch 2—24 hdc + 16 pf + 8 ch-1 spaces.

Round 15: Ch 1, 1 sc in each of the next 4 sts, 1 sc in next ch space, *1 sc in each of the next 5 sts, 1 sc in next ch space; repeat from * around; 1 sc in last st, sl st to join to 1st sc—48 sc.

Round 16: 1 sl st in each st around, do not join—48 sl st.

Round 17: Ch 1, 1 sc in each st around working into round 15, sl st to join to 1st sc—48 sc.

Round 18: Repeat round 16.

Round 19: Ch 1, 1 sc in each st around working into round 18, invisible join to 1st sc, and fasten off—48 sc.

Underground Beanie

Underground Beanie

A big-ribbed beanie is quick to whip up and sure to keep you warm! Fold the edge up for a classic beanie style or wear it unfolded if you prefer some slouch.

YARN
Red Heart Soft Essentials, #5 bulky weight yarn, acrylic, 5 oz (141 g) per skein: 150 (180) yd / 137 (165) m of #7851 Navy

MATERIALS
» US Size K/10.5 (6.5 mm) crochet hook or size needed to obtain gauge
» Yarn needle
» Scissors

DIFFICULTY
Easy

SIZES
Small (Large)

FINISHED MEASUREMENTS
Small:
    Length: 10.5 in (27 cm)
    Circumference: 21 in (53 cm)
Large:
    Length: 11.5 in (29 cm)
    Circumference: 22 in (56 cm)

GAUGE
11 dc/FPdc and 7 rows of pattern = 4 in (10 cm)

NOTES
» Hat is worked flat in rows and then stitched together to form a tube. Top will be cinched shut at the end.
» Pattern is written for size Small with adjustments for size Large in parentheses.

INSTRUCTIONS

Row 1 (RS): Ch 29 (34), 1 sc in 2nd ch from hook, 1 sc in each of the next 2 chs, 1 hdc in each of the next 3 chs, 1 dc in each of the next 22 (27) chs—3 sc + 3 hdc + 22 dc (3 sc + 3 hdc + 27 dc).

Row 2: Ch 2 (counts as 1 FPdc) and turn, 1 FPdc in each of the next 21 (26) sts, 1 FPhdc in each of the next 3 sts, 1 FPsc in each of the next 3 sts—3 FPsc + 3 FPhdc + 22 FPdc (3 FPsc + 3 FPhdc + 27 FPdc).

Row 3: Ch 1 (counts as 1 sc) and turn, 1 sc in each of the next 2 sts, 1 hdc in each of the next 3 sts, 1 dc in each of the next 22 (27) sts—3 sc + 3 hdc + 22 dc (3 sc + 3 hdc + 27 dc).

Rows 4–31 (4–33): Repeat rows 2–3.

Row 32 (34): Repeat row 2.

Cut yarn, leaving a long tail. Using yarn needle and the tail, stitch final row to beginning chain to form a tube, and fasten off.

Using yarn needle and a scrap of yarn, stitch around the end of the tube. Pull tight to cinch the end shut, and fasten off.

Manhattan Beanie

This lighter-weight beanie features stripes that incorporate spike stitches to create a classic, sporty style. Finish it off with a nice ribbed edging and a two-tone pom-pom on top!

YARN
Knit Picks Wool of the Andes, #4 medium worsted weight yarn, wool, 2 oz (50 g) per skein: 90 yd (82 m) of #23898 Lake Ice Heather (**A**), 65 yd (59 m) of #24653 Calypso Heather (**B**), and 65 yd (59 m) of #23899 Sapphire Heather (**C**)

MATERIALS
» US Size I/9 (5.5 mm) crochet hook or size needed to obtain gauge
» Stitch marker
» Pom-pom maker
» Yarn needle
» Scissors

DIFFICULTY
Easy

SIZES
One size

FINISHED MEASUREMENTS
Length: 8 in (20 cm)
Circumference: 24 in (61 cm)

GAUGE
16 sc and 16 rows = 4 in (10 cm)

SPECIAL STITCHES
Spike single crochet (ssc): Insert hook in st below next st, yo, draw up a loop to the height of the current round, yo, draw through both loops on hook.

NOTES

» Pattern is worked in continuous rounds until round 31. Rounds 31–33 will be joined at the end of each round.

» Use a stitch marker to keep track of the beginning of rounds.

» Carry each color up to minimize the number of cut ends.

INSTRUCTIONS

With **A**, make a magic ring.

Round 1: Ch 1 (does not count as a st), 6 sc in ring—6 sc.

Round 2: 2 sc in each st around—12 sc.

Round 3: *1 sc in the next st, 2 sc in the next st; repeat from * around—18 sc.

Round 4: *1 sc in each of the next 2 sts, 2 sc in the next st; repeat from * around—24 sc.

Round 5: *1 sc in each of the next 3 sts, 2 sc in the next st; repeat from * around—30 sc.

Round 6: *1 sc in each of the next 4 sts, 2 sc in the next st; repeat from * around—36 sc.

Round 7: *1 sc in each of the next 5 sts, 2 sc in the next st; repeat from * around—42 sc.

Round 8: *1 sc in each of the next 6 sts, 2 sc in the next st; repeat from * around—48 sc.

Round 9: *1 sc in each of the next 7 sts, 2 sc in the next st; repeat from * around—54 sc.

Round 10: *1 sc in each of the next 8 sts, 2 sc in the next st; repeat from * around—60 sc.

Round 11: *1 sc in each of the next 9 sts, 2 sc in the next st; repeat from * around—66 sc.

Round 12: *1 sc in each of the next 10 sts, 2 sc in the next st; repeat from * around—72 sc.

Round 13: With **B**, *1 ssc in next st, 1 sc in next st; repeat from * around—36 ssc + 36 sc.

Round 14: 1 sc in each st around—72 sc.

Round 15: With **C**, *1 ssc in next st, 1 sc in next st; repeat from * around—36 ssc + 36 sc.

Round 16: 1 sc in each st around—72 sc.

Round 17: With **A**, *1 ssc in next st, 1 sc in next st; repeat from * around—36 ssc + 36 sc.

Round 18: 1 sc in each st around—72 sc.

Rounds 19–30: Repeat rounds 13–18, 2 times.

Round 31: With **A**, ch 2 (counts as 1 dc), 1 dc in each st around, sl st to top of ch 2 to join—72 dc.

Round 32: Ch 3 (counts as 1 dc), 1 FPdc in next st, *1 dc in next st, 1 FPdc in next st; repeat from * around, sl st to top of ch 3 to join—36 dc + 36 FPdc.

Round 33: Ch 3 (counts as 1 dc), 1 FPdc in next st, *1 dc in next st, 1 FPdc in next st; repeat from * around, invisible join to top of ch 3 and fasten off—36 dc + 36 FPdc.

FINISHING

Attach a pom-pom to the top of the hat if desired.

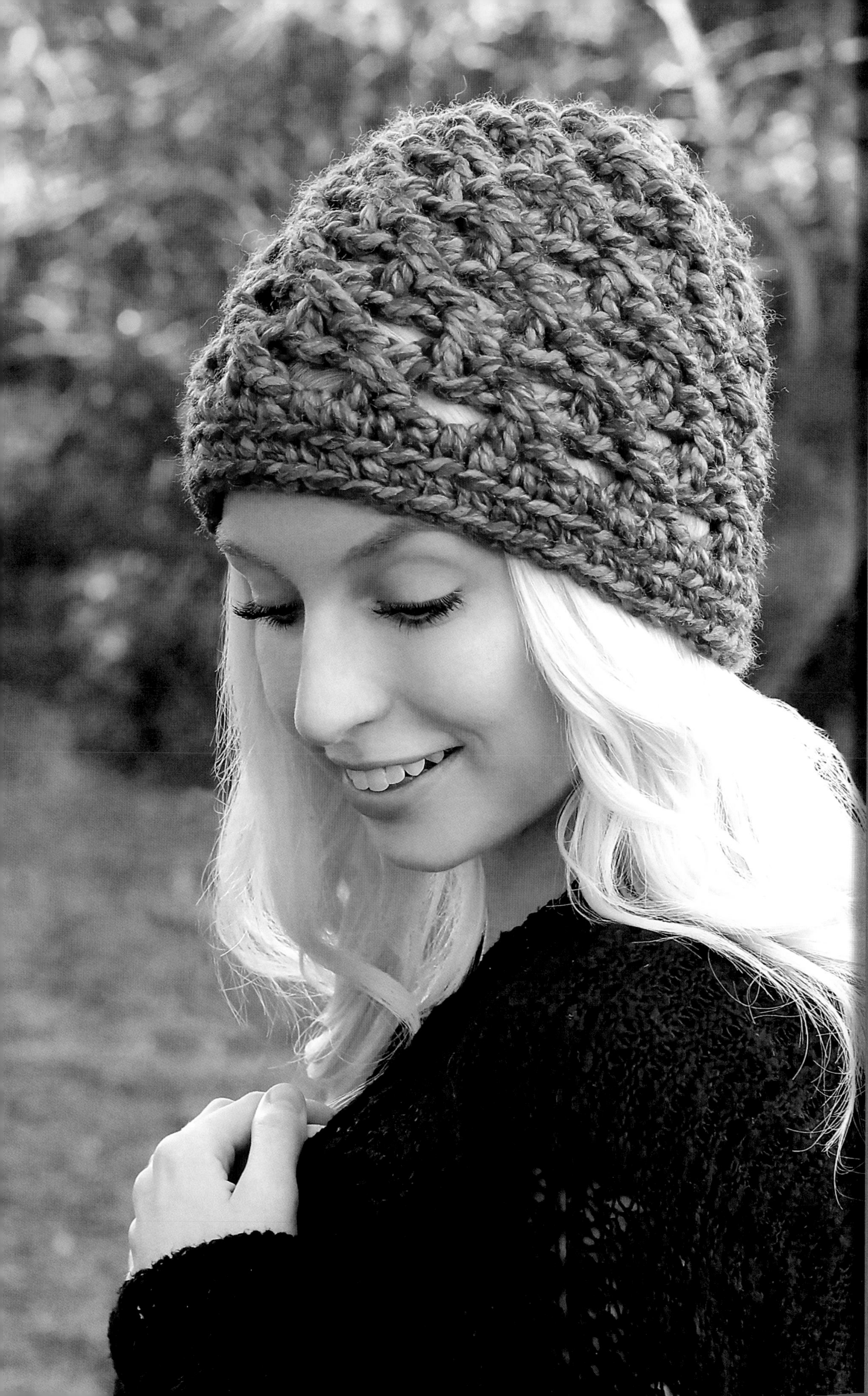

Twist Beanie

Twist Beanie

This super bulky beanie is a quick one-skein project. Crossing stitches creates a twisted texture and small openings for a unique look.

YARN
Lion Brand Wool-Ease Thick and Quick, #6 super bulky weight yarn, acrylic/wool, 6 oz (170 g) per skein: 75 yd (69 m) of #525 Wild Strawberry

MATERIALS
» US Size N/13 (9 mm) crochet hook or size needed to obtain gauge
» Yarn needle
» Scissors

DIFFICULTY
Easy

SIZES
One size

FINISHED MEASUREMENTS
Length: 8.5 in (22 cm)
Circumference: 22 in (56 cm)

GAUGE
[skip 2 dc, 1 dc in next dc, ch 1, 1 dc in previous dc, ch 1] 2 times and 12 hdc and 4 rows = 3½ in (9 cm)

NOTES
» Ch 4 at beginning of rounds will always count as 1 dc + 1 ch.
» Ch 1 at beginning of rounds will always count as 1 sc.

INSTRUCTIONS

Make a magic ring.

Round 1: Ch 4 (counts as 1 dc + 1 ch now and throughout), [1 dc in ring, ch 1] 11 times, sl st to 3rd ch to join—12 dc + 12 ch-1 spaces.

Round 2: Ch 4, 1 dc in dc before ch 4, ch 1, skip st where ch 4 was made, 1 dc in next dc, ch 1, 1 dc in same st as ch 4, ch 1, *skip dc where previous dc was made, 1 dc in next dc, ch 1, 1 dc in previous dc, ch 1; repeat from * around, sl st to 3rd ch to join—24 dc + 24 ch-1 spaces.

Rounds 3–8: Ch 4, 1 dc in dc before ch 4, ch 1, skip st where ch 4 was made and next dc, 1 dc in next dc, ch 1, 1 dc in previous dc, ch 1, *skip st where dc was made and next dc, 1 dc in next dc, ch 1, 1 dc in previous dc, ch 1; repeat from * around, sl st to 3rd ch to join—24 dc + 24 ch-1 spaces.

Round 9: Ch 1 (counts as 1 sc now and throughout), 1 sc in next ch space, *1 sc in next dc, 1 sc in next ch space; repeat from * around, sl st to 1st sc to join—48 sc.

Round 10: Ch 1, 1 BLO sc in each st, invisible join to 1st sc, and fasten off—48 sc.

Cinnamon Swirl Slouchy Beanie

Cinnamon Swirl Slouchy Beanie

This slouchy beanie is made in a continuous spiral that will remind you of a cinnamon bun! Using a multicolored yarn will create easy stripes without the need to change colors.

YARN
Red Heart Unforgettable, #4 medium worsted weight yarn, acrylic, 3.5 oz (100 g) per skein: 190 (210) yd /178 (192) m of #9942 Cappuccino

MATERIALS
» US Size H/8 (5 mm) crochet hook or size needed to obtain gauge
» Measuring tape
» Yarn needle
» Scissors
» Stitch marker

DIFFICULTY
Easy

SIZES
Small (Large)

FINISHED MEASUREMENTS
Small:
Length: 10 in (25 cm)
Circumference: 20 in (51 cm)
Large:
Length: 12 in (30 cm)
Circumference: 22 in (56 cm)

GAUGE
16 dc worked in third loop and 8 rows = 4 in (10 cm)

NOTES

» Pattern is worked in continuous rounds. Starting with round 2, you will need to use a stitch marker to mark the beginning of rounds.

» Starting with round 2, all stitches will be made in the third loop.

» Pattern is written for size Small with adjustments for size Large in parentheses.

INSTRUCTIONS

Make a magic ring.

Round 1: Ch 3 (counts as 1 dc), 12 dc in ring—13 dc.

Round 2: 2 dc in top of ch 3 from beginning of previous round and work all sts in 3rd loop from here on, 2 dc in each st around—26 dc.

Round 3: *1 dc in next st, 2 dc in next st; repeat from * around—39 dc.

Round 4: *1 dc in each of the next 2 sts, 2 dc in next st; repeat from * around—52 dc.

Round 5: *1 dc in each of the next 3 sts, 2 dc in next st; repeat from * around—65 dc.

Round 6 (size Large only): *1 dc in each of the next 4 sts, 2 dc in next st; repeat from * around—78 dc.

Rounds 6–20 (7–22): 1 dc in each st around—65 (78) dc.

Round 21 (23): 1 dc in each of the next 59 (72) sts, 1 hdc in each of the next 3 sts, 1 sc in each of the next 3 sts, invisible join to third loop of next st, and fasten off—59 (72) dc + 3 hdc + 3 sc.

Raspberry Beanie

Raspberry Beanie

This warm beanie is made with super bulky yarn, using puff stitches to create a raspberry-like texture. Finish it off with long ties and large pom-poms just for fun!

YARN
Loops and Threads Cozy Wool, #6 super bulky weight yarn, wool/acrylic, 4.5 oz (127 g) per skein: 130 yd (119 m) of #02430 Merlot

MATERIALS
» US Size P/15 (10 mm) crochet hook or size needed to obtain gauge
» Yarn needle
» Scissors
» Pom-pom maker

DIFFICULTY
Easy

SIZES
One size

FINISHED MEASUREMENTS
Length: 9 in (23 cm)
Circumference: 22 in (56 cm)

GAUGE
7 pf and 6 rows = 6 in (15 cm)

SPECIAL STITCHES
Puff (pf): [Yo, insert hook into stitch, yo and pull up a loop] 3 times, yo and pull through all 7 loops on hook.

NOTES
» Pattern is worked in joined rounds with the exception of row 10, which is not a full round.
» Ch 2 and ch 1 in beginning of rounds will not count as sts.

INSTRUCTIONS

Make a magic ring.

Round 1: Ch 2 (does not count as a st now and throughout), 7 pf in ring, sl st to join to 1st pf—7 pf.

Round 2: Ch 2, 2 pf in each st around, sl st to join to 1st pf—14 pf.

Round 3: Ch 2, *1 pf in next st, 2 pf in next st; repeat from * around, sl st to join to 1st pf—21 pf.

Round 4: Ch 2, *1 pf in each of the next 2 sts, 2 pf in next st; repeat from * around, sl st to join to 1st pf—28 pf.

Rounds 5–8: Ch 2, 1 pf in each st around, sl st to join to 1st pf—28 pf.

Round 9: Ch 1 (does not count as a st), 1 sc in each st around, invisible join to 1st sc, and fasten off—28 sc.

Row 10: Ch 20, skip 6 sts after invisible join, 1 dc in each of the next 16 sts, ch 20, fasten off—16 dc + 40 chs.

FINISHING

Make 2 pom-poms, leaving a tail attached to each. Use yarn needle and the tail to attach 1 pom-pom to the end of each ch in row 10.

Stitches and Techniques

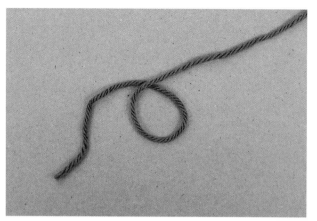

1. Loop yarn as shown to make a ring a few inches from the end of the yarn.

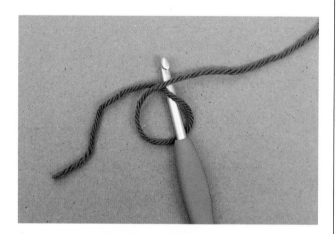

2. Insert hook into the ring, yarn over, and draw up a loop.

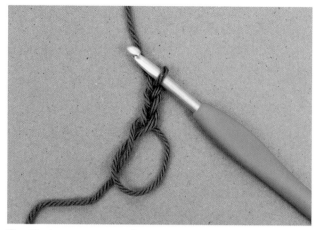

3. Chain as instructed in pattern (3 ch shown).

4. Crochet into ring, working over both pieces of yarn.

5. Pull tail to close ring.

Front Loop Only (FLO), Back Loop Only (BLO), Third Loop

At the top of each stitch you will see two loops. The front loop is closest to you and the back loop is behind it. If you flip your work over, the loop right below the back loop is known as the third loop. Normally, stitches are made into both front and back loops. When a pattern instructs you to work into a specific loop only, you will ignore the other loops and insert your hook only into the loop specified while crocheting.

The needle is through the third loop (note that the crochet piece is showing the wrong side of the fabric).

Slip Stitch (sl st)

Insert hook into stitch, yarn over, and draw up a loop through the stitch and the loop on hook.

The needle is through the front loop.

The needle is through the back loop.

Single Crochet (sc)

1. Insert hook into stitch.

2. Yarn over and draw up a loop.

3. Yarn over and draw through two loops.

Single Crochet 2 Together (sc2tog)

1. Insert hook into stitch.

2. Yarn over and draw up a loop.

3. Insert hook into next stitch.

4. Yarn over and draw up a loop.

5. Yarn over and draw through all three loops.

1. Insert hook behind stitch.

2. Yarn over and draw up a loop.

3. Yarn over and draw through two loops.

Spike Single Crochet (ssc)

1. Insert hook into stitch below next stitch.

2. Yarn over and draw up a loop to the height of the current round.

3. Yarn over and draw through both loops on hook.

Half Double Crochet (hdc)

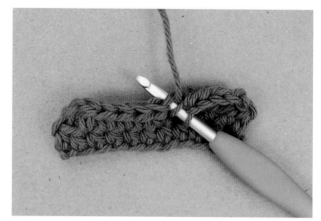

1. Yarn over and insert hook into stitch.

2. Yarn over and draw up a loop.

3. Yarn over and draw through all three loops.

Half Double Crochet 2 Together (hdc2tog)

1. Yarn over and insert hook into stitch.

2. Yarn over and draw up a loop.

3. Yarn over and insert hook into next stitch.

4. Yarn over and draw up a loop.

5. Yarn over and draw through all five loops.

Front Post Half Double Crochet (FPhdc)

1. Yarn over and insert hook behind stitch.

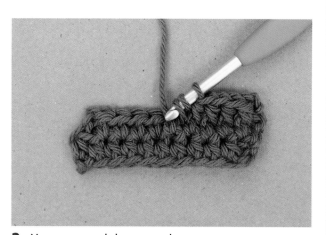

2. Yarn over and draw up a loop.

3. Yarn over and draw through all three loops.

Double Crochet (dc)

1. Yarn over and insert hook into stitch.

2. Yarn over and draw up a loop.

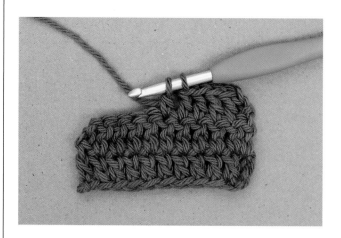

3. [Yarn over and draw through two loops] twice.

Double Crochet 2 Together (dc2tog)

1. Yarn over and insert hook into stitch.

2. Yarn over and draw up a loop.

3. Yarn over and draw through two loops.

4. Yarn over and insert hook into next stitch.

5. Yarn over and draw up a loop.

2. Yarn over and draw up a loop.

6. [Yarn over and draw through two loops] twice.

Front Post Double Crochet (FPdc)

3. [Yarn over and draw through two loops] twice.

1. Yarn over and insert hook behind stitch.

Treble Crochet (tr)

1. Yarn over twice and insert hook into stitch.

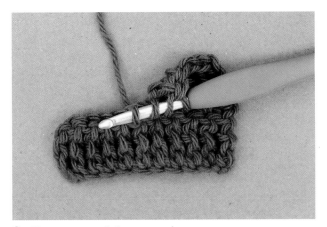

2. Yarn over and draw up a loop.

3. [Yarn over and draw through two loops] three times.

Front Post Treble Crochet (FPtr)

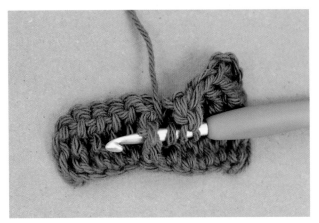

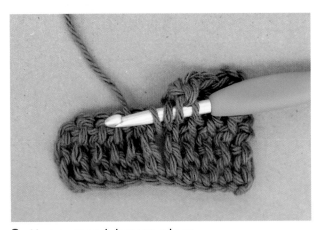

1. Yarn over twice and insert hook behind stitch.

2. Yarn over and draw up a loop.

3. [Yarn over and draw through two loops] three times.

Puff (pf)

1. [Yarn over and insert hook into stitch, yarn over and draw up a loop] three times.

2. [Yarn over and insert hook into stitch] three times.

3. Yarn over and draw through all seven loops on hook.

4 dc Bobble (bo)

1. [Yarn over and insert hook into stitch, yarn over and draw up a loop, yarn over and draw through two loops] four times.

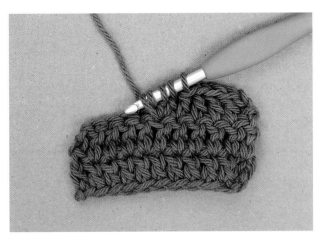

2. Yarn over and draw through all five loops on hook.

5 dc Bobble (bo)

1. [Yarn over and insert hook into stitch, yarn over and draw up a loop, yarn over and draw through two loops] five times. See step 1 for 4 dc Bobble for photos; repeat five times for the 5 dc Bobble.

2. Yarn over and draw through all six loops on hook.

Color Change in Continuous (nonjoined) Rounds

The stitch before the color change should be started with the original color and then completed with the new color. The example shown here is with single crochets.

1. Insert hook into stitch.

2. Yarn over and draw up a loop.

3. Yarn over with new color and draw through both loops.

4. Continue working with new color.

After completing the final stitch of the round with the original color, the slip stitch will then be made with the new color. The example shown is with double crochets.

1. Insert hook into top of chain at beginning of round.

2. Yarn over with new color and draw through the stitch and the loop on hook.

3. Continue working with new color.

1. After final stitch of the round, cut yarn leaving a small tail and pull up through stitch.

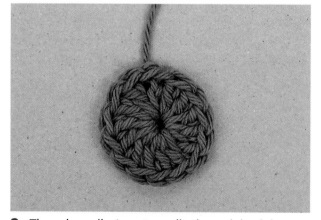

2. Thread needle, insert needle through both loops of first stitch of the round, and pull through to the back.

3. Insert needle through back loop only of final stitch of the round, pull through to the back, and fasten off.

Whipstitching to Form a Tube

When a hat is worked in rows, you will need to stitch the first row to the last row to form a tube.

1. Thread needle with a piece of yarn and fold hat in half so that first and last rows are touching, insert needle through a stitch in the first and last rows, and pull through. Note: contrasting yarn was used here for illustration purposes only.

2. Repeat, working toward the other end of the hat, and then fasten off.

Cinching Top of Hat Shut

Some hats will need to be cinched shut at the top.

1. Thread your needle with a piece of yarn; insert needle into a stitch and pull through. Note: contrasting yarn was used here for illustration purposes only.

2. Repeat for several stitches.

3. Pull on yarn to cinch those stitches together.

4. Repeat for another several stitches at a time until you've made it all the way around the top of the hat. Pull yarn to cinch the hat completely shut, insert needle into inside of hat, and fasten off.

Abbreviations

BegBo	beginning bobble
BLO	back loop only
bo	bobble
ch(s)	chain(s)
dc	double crochet
dc2tog	double crochet 2 together
FLO	front loop only
FPdc	front post double crochet
FPhdc	front post half double crochet
FPsc	front post single crochet
FPtr	front post treble crochet
hdc	half double crochet
hdc2tog	half double crochet 2 together
pf	puff
RS	right side
sc	single crochet
sl st	slip stitch
ssc	spike single crochet
st(s)	stitch(es)
tr	treble crochet
yo	yarn over

Resources

YARN

Bernat
yarnspirations.com

Loops and Threads
michaels.com

Caron
yarnspirations.com

Patons
yarnspirations.com

Cascade
cascadeyarns.com

Premier
premieryarns.com

Knit Picks
knitpicks.com

Red Heart
redheart.com

Lion Brand
lionbrand.com

Yarn Bee
hobbylobby.com

TOOLS AND EMBELLISHMENTS

Clover (clover-usa.com)
Hooks, yarn needles, stitch markers, pom-pom maker, tassel maker

Etsy (etsy.com)
Faux fur pom-poms

Joann (joann.com)
Buttons, ribbon

Acknowledgments

Thank you to all of my family and friends who have cheered me on through the long process of creating this book. Thank you for always encouraging my creativity and tolerating my frequent "Look what I made!" moments. Thank you, also, for happily adopting so many of these hats!

Thank you to all of my amazing pattern testers for the time you've dedicated to these patterns and your willingness to make *so* many hats! I always appreciate your attention to detail, suggestions, and enthusiasm over new designs. This book is better because of you.

Thank you to everyone at Stackpole for all that you've done behind the scenes to bring this book to life. Thank you, Candi, for all of your help and patience. I very much appreciate the opportunity to write this book.

Thank you to my beautiful models, Tiffani, Brooke, and Kaity, for being so wonderful to work with. I appreciate your help with styling outfits and am happy that, as I flip through this book and see your smiling faces, I'll be reminded of how fun the photo shoots were!

Thank you to Cascade, Knit Picks, Lion Brand, Premier, Red Heart, and Yarnspirations for so generously providing yarn to use in designing these hats. These are some of my favorite yarns, so it was a pleasure to include them.

Thank you to my friends and followers in the online crochet community who have shown enthusiasm for this book. I designed these hats with you in mind and hope you will enjoy making and wearing them!

Visual Index

Seashell Slouchy Hat 2

Lakeshore Beanie 5

Diamonds Slouchy Hat 8

Pumpkin Pie Slouchy Beanie 11

Stained Glass Slouchy Beanie 15

Ferris Wheel Slouchy Hat 18

Swell Slouchy Beanie 22

Twinkle Slouchy Beanie 25

Ginger Snap Slouchy Hat 28

Spring Blossom Slouchy Hat 32

Skate Date Beanie 35

Avenue C Slouchy Hat 38

Ivy Slouchy Beanie 41

Amethyst Slouchy Hat 44

Pineapple Coconut
Slouchy Hat 47

Heartbeat Slouchy Hat 50

September Slouchy Hat 53

Cottontail Beanie 56

Festival Slouchy Hat 59

Alaska Beanie 62

High Tide Beanie 65